HOME COOKING

with

WILD GAME

STEVE & ANNIE CHAPMAN

TEN PEAKS PRESS®
EUGENE, OR

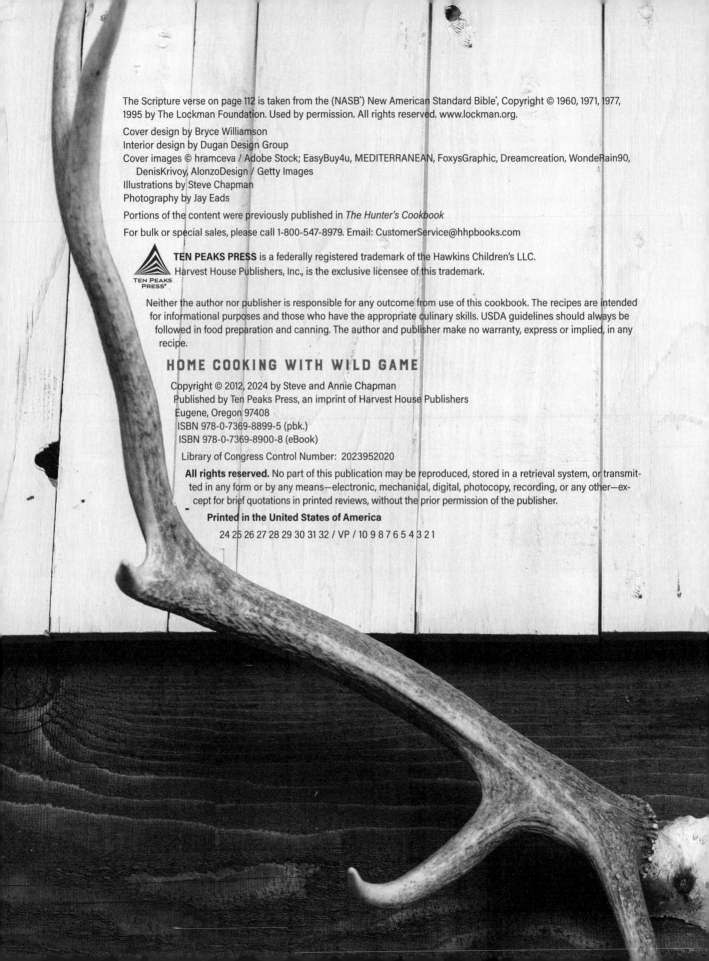

The Scripture verse on page 112 is taken from the (NASB®) New American Standard Bible®, Copyright © 1960, 1971, 1977, 1995 by The Lockman Foundation. Used by permission. All rights reserved. www.lockman.org.

Cover design by Bryce Williamson

Interior design by Dugan Design Group

Cover images © hramceva / Adobe Stock; EasyBuy4u, MEDITERRANEAN, FoxysGraphic, Dreamcreation, WondeRain90, DenisKrivoy, AlonzoDesign / Getty Images

Illustrations by Steve Chapman

Photography by Jay Eads

Portions of the content were previously published in *The Hunter's Cookbook*

For bulk or special sales, please call 1-800-547-8979. Email: CustomerService@hhpbooks.com

TEN PEAKS PRESS is a federally registered trademark of the Hawkins Children's LLC. Harvest House Publishers, Inc., is the exclusive licensee of this trademark.

Neither the author nor publisher is responsible for any outcome from use of this cookbook. The recipes are intended for informational purposes and those who have the appropriate culinary skills. USDA guidelines should always be followed in food preparation and canning. The author and publisher make no warranty, express or implied, in any recipe.

HOME COOKING WITH WILD GAME

Copyright © 2012, 2024 by Steve and Annie Chapman

Published by Ten Peaks Press, an imprint of Harvest House Publishers

Eugene, Oregon 97408

ISBN 978-0-7369-8899-5 (pbk.)

ISBN 978-0-7369-8900-8 (eBook)

Library of Congress Control Number: 2023952020

All rights reserved. No part of this publication may be reproduced, stored in a retrieval system, or transmitted in any form or by any means—electronic, mechanical, digital, photocopy, recording, or any other—except for brief quotations in printed reviews, without the prior permission of the publisher.

Printed in the United States of America

24 25 26 27 28 29 30 31 32 / VP / 10 9 8 7 6 5 4 3 2 1

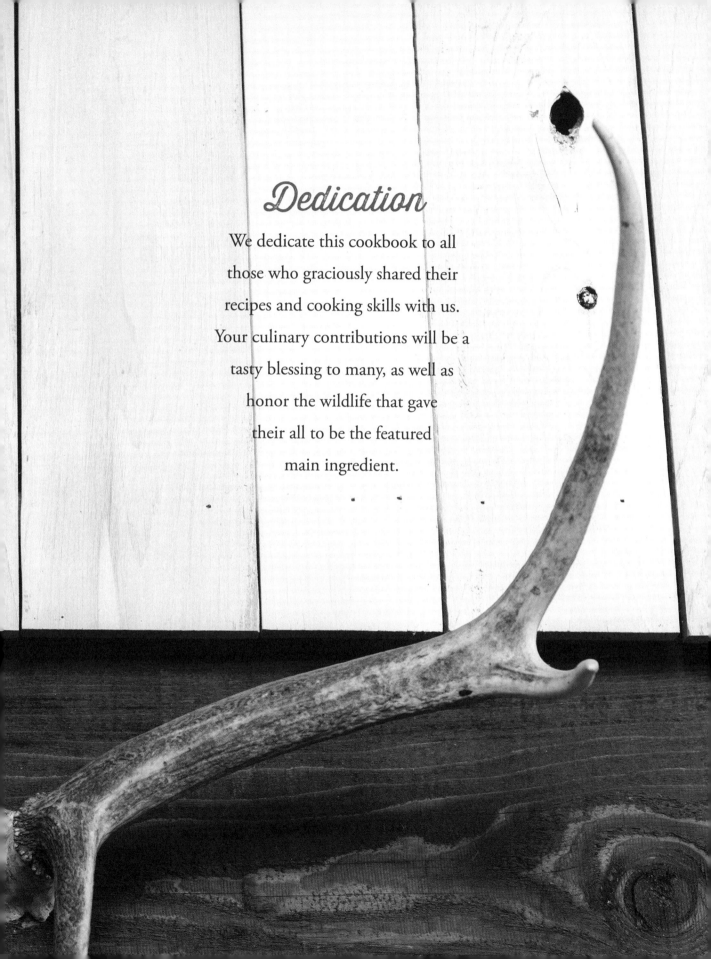

Dedication

We dedicate this cookbook to all
those who graciously shared their
recipes and cooking skills with us.
Your culinary contributions will be a
tasty blessing to many, as well as
honor the wildlife that gave
their all to be the featured
main ingredient.

Contents

Introduction

BY ANNIE

Home Cooking with Wild Game was a welcomed writing project for Steve and me. For several years Steve had been busy writing books to inspire men with the insights he'd gleaned from the outdoors, while I'd been occupied with addressing topics that appeal to women. Now, we get to be a writing team.

Steve's eagerness to work on this book was on the tip of his fingers. He's always looking for a reason to pen more stories about hunting and fishing. I chuckle at what he usually says when he heads out the door to enjoy a deer hunt or go to a lake with his rod and reel: "Hey, babe, I'm off to do more book research!"

My enthusiasm for this writing came easy for two reasons. First, it is a pleasure to provide a collection of wild game recipes we've enjoyed through the years. The main dishes favored by our family (and relatives, friends, and friends of friends) include mostly venison, elk, and turkey, so those sections contain more entries. Thankfully, other contributors' palates range wider, so we've included some of their favorite recipes for other species.

The second reason I gladly got involved has much to do with growing up on a farm in West Virginia. Although my childhood included a few more creature comforts than my parents had growing up (a fancier woodstove, more efficient water pump, and eventually indoor plumbing), I still recall a time when self-sufficiency was a necessary way of life. For example, our family lived quite a distance from a well-stocked grocery store, and there certainly were no restaurants close by. Our trips to town were limited to occasional runs for staples, such as flour and sugar. For the most part, the rest of our shopping was done in our garden.

In my younger years, we didn't have a refrigerator or freezer, so we canned and cured our vegetables and meats...or ate them before they spoiled. Except in the winter when there may have been a spare hog or steer to butcher and the occasional barnyard chicken to chase down and prepare, much of the animal protein our family enjoyed came from the woods, fields, and streams of the farmland around us via the hunting and fishing skills of my dad and, later, my brothers.

From deer to grouse, from squirrels to catfish, the range of consumable critters was intensely valued. Without the harvest of the land, we wouldn't have been as nourished as we were, especially during the leaner economic times.

Because of my deep appreciation for the natural resources God provides that helped sustain my parents, my five siblings, and me, I'm excited about offering a book that will help you appreciate and utilize the bounty of the land. I sincerely hope you will find this book a useful resource for savoring the rewards of the hunt. The hunting and fishing stories Steve has included, which I suggest you read aloud during dinner, give an added dimension to this cookbook that is unique and entertaining. May all the information be used to bless those who put their feet under your table.

Part One

BIG GAME

Venison

In the early 1900s, the white-tailed deer population was thought to be as low as 500,000 in North America. Thankfully conservation and good hunting regulations have helped increase and sustain the population at healthy levels. Estimates today have the overall herd at more than 20 million, plenty of deer to do their part in nature's life cycle, to let us enjoy watching them, and to allow us to safely harvest some for our tables. Along with the joy of the fair chase, I (Steve) thoroughly enjoy the other benefit hunting brings, as evidenced in this little poem I wrote several years ago.

THE RECIPE

I saw the deer and took its life
     Then gave it to my skillful wife
She added leeks and tall morels
     A secret spice I dare not tell
And deep-red fruit of tomato vines
     Legumes and fire and evening time
Bread of wheat and coffee hot...
     She made me glad I took the shot

What a wonderful food source God has given us in the deer! One of the advantages of using venison is the lack of fat content. If you're interested in keeping your diet healthy and nutritious, then deer meat is a viable alternative.

A good hunting buddy of mine had heart bypass surgery. He said he feared that the nutritionist in charge of tweaking his diet would eliminate his favorite meat. Much to his delight, she said he could eat all the venison he wanted. It's considered heart friendly.

So whether whitetail, mule deer, coastal black-tail, or any of the imported exotics, we can be grateful for the sustenance they provide. And there might be as many ways to prepare deer for consumption as there are deer to consume! The following recipes have been enjoyed by many over the years.

We hope you enjoy them too.

 **VENISON COOKING TIPS**

- An important key to a good venison meal is to make sure the raw meat is prepared correctly. Clean away all fat, silver skin (the white membrane), tendons, and connective tissue. Remove the bones. Never cut into the bone when deboning or preparing venison. Cut around the bone to remove the meat. Put the carefully cleaned meat in a large bowl of cold water with a generous amount of salt. Cover and place in the refrigerator. Let the meat sit for a few hours (even a day), and then drain. Rinse the salt off. Now it's ready to freeze or cook.

- Never freeze wild big game in plastic wrap. Several layers of freezer paper will help to avoid freezer burn, which venison is especially susceptible to because of its low fat, high water content. Be sure to date the freezer packages and use meat within eight months.

- To avoid any gamy taste, let the meat thaw slowly in the refrigerator. This may take a couple of days. Never use hot water to hurry the thawing process. If you need to quickly thaw the meat, leave the venison in the freezer paper and let it sit in cold water.

- There are two basic cuts of meat to be used in preparing venison. The more tender cuts of meat come from muscles that are not used a lot, including the back (the coveted back tenderloin called backstrap) and parts of the legs. These cuts should not be overcooked and can be prepared rather quickly. The cuts that come from the deer's working muscles, the ones used vigorously in the life of the animal, should be cooked at a lower temperature and for a longer period of time for best results. A Crock-Pot is ideal.

- Because of its lack of grease, venison tends to dry out. One remedy is to use a moist cooking method, such as stewing, braising, or boiling. When cooking meat that tends to be less tender, be sure to cook it longer and more slowly. A Crock-Pot is a perfect solution when preparing these cuts of meat. Add a packet of dry soup mix with some water and onion, and you will not be disappointed.

- If you use a dry-cooking method (grilling or broiling), be sure to reduce the cooking time. Cook the meat less well done than you might otherwise and baste the meat while it cooks so it won't dry out.

- Venison should be served immediately after grilling. If you let the meat cool, the fiber in the muscles will firm up and the meat will be less tender.

- How can you be sure wild game meat is done? Use the fork tender method. If you can cut it easily with a fork, it's done.

- When frying with butter, make sure the heat isn't so hot that it burns the butter.

- When frying with oil, remember that really hot oil causes the meat to tighten and become less tender.

VENISON STROGANOFF DELIGHT

Ingredients

1 lb. ground venison

1 medium onion, thinly sliced

8 oz. mushrooms, cleaned
and stemmed

1 clove garlic, minced

2 T. olive oil

1 T. Worcestershire sauce

1 (12 oz.) pkg. egg noodles

1 (10.5 oz.) can cream of
mushroom soup

1 (10.5 oz.) can beef broth

½ cup sour cream

1 (2 oz.) packet beef and
mushroom dry soup mix

Directions

Cook venison and drain in colander, removing as much fat as possible. (If desired, you can rinse it under warm water to remove more fat.) Place meat in a 6-quart pan and set aside.

In a skillet, sauté onion, mushroom, and garlic in olive oil. Add Worcestershire sauce and simmer.

Prepare egg noodles according to package instructions. Drain and set aside.

Whisk soup, broth, sour cream, and dry soup mix in a bowl. Stir mixture into meat and bring to boil. Immediately reduce heat and simmer uncovered for a few minutes.

Serve hot over the egg noodles.

Tip: With the meat and starch taken care of, add a green salad and supper is ready!

VENISON BURGER CASSEROLE

Ingredients

1 lb. ground venison

1 (8 oz.) pkg. egg noodles

1 cup chopped celery

1 cup chopped onion

3 cloves garlic, minced

1 cup diced green bell pepper

4 T. butter

1 (15 oz.) can tomato sauce

1 tsp. salt

¼ tsp. black pepper

1 cup shredded cheddar cheese

Directions

Preheat oven to 350°.

Cook and drain the venison.

Prepare egg noodles according to package instructions. Drain and set aside.

Sauté celery, onion, garlic, and bell pepper in butter. Add tomato sauce, salt, and pepper and stir. Add egg noodles to mixture and stir. Place into oven-safe casserole dish.

Bake for 30 to 40 minutes. Make sure it is nice and bubbly all over.

Cover meat mixture with cheese and put back into the oven until the cheese is melted.

Tip: This casserole usually feeds 6.

STIR-FRY VENISON

Ingredients

1 lb. venison backstrap or steak

Nonstick cooking spray

1 T. olive oil

1 large onion, chopped

1 bell pepper, thinly sliced

3 cloves garlic, minced

1 T. Worcestershire sauce (gluten free optional)

1 tsp. hot sauce

1 tsp. cornstarch

¼ cup water

2 cups cooked rice

Directions

Cut venison into strips. (Venison is easier to cut if partially frozen.)

Coat a wok with cooking spray or use a heavy, lightly greased skillet. Add oil and heat on medium high until hot. Add venison and stir-fry 1 minute. Add vegetables and stir-fry until veggies reach desired tenderness. Now add sauces and mix well.

In a separate bowl, mix the cornstarch and water. Add to meat and vegetables, stirring constantly until mixture thickens.

Serve over rice.

Tip: This recipe usually feeds 4 people.

BEST EVER VENISON ROAST

Ingredients

3 lbs. venison roast

Salt

Pepper

Garlic powder

1 cup flour

3 T. oil

1 large onion, coarsely chopped

1 (28 oz.) can crushed tomatoes

1 cup water

Hot sauce to taste

Directions

Trim the roast of visible fat. Score the roast with thin cuts on the diagonal to help the meat be more tender. Sprinkle all sides of meat with salt, pepper, and garlic powder. Dredge in flour.

Pour oil in frying pan and heat until hot. Carefully place roast in oil and brown on all sides.

Remove meat from frying pan and place in roaster or covered pan.

Put the remaining ingredients on the meat and place in oven.

Bake at 300° for 3 hours or until done.

Serves 10 to 12 people.

Tip: Use the drippings to make Poor Man's Gravy (page 186).

VENISON MEATBALLS

Ingredients

2 lbs. ground venison

Nonstick cooking spray, for skillet

1 (2 oz.) packet onion soup mix

1 cup ketchup

1½ cups water

¼ tsp. garlic powder

1 tsp. oregano

1 T. Worcestershire sauce

Directions

Preheat oven to 350°. Form ground venison into meatballs. Brown them in a lightly greased skillet. Remove from stove.

Mix remaining ingredients together. Pour sauce over meatballs and put into oven.

Bake for 1 hour or until done.

Tip: Serve with spaghetti and toasted Italian bread.

VENISON MEATBALLS SUPREME

Ingredients

½ lb. ground venison

1 lb. ground round hamburger

1 can water chestnuts, drained and diced

¾ cup fine dry breadcrumbs

1 tsp. Worcestershire sauce

1 tsp. parsley

1 egg

1½ tsp. salt

⅛ tsp. pepper

½ cup milk

Sauce

1 (13.5 oz.) bottle ketchup

1 (10.5 oz.) jar currant jelly

Directions

Meatballs

Preheat oven to 350°. Mix together all ingredients and roll into walnut-size balls.

Bake on ungreased cookie sheet for 40 minutes.

Sauce

In a large saucepan, heat ketchup and jelly together and bring to a boil.

Pour over meatballs and heat again, simmering until the meatballs and sauce are bubbly and all the flavors have mingled.

Serve hot or at room temperature. This is a great party food. Serve with toothpicks.

Tip: Venison tastes best when it is served in a combination of sweet and salty flavors. The currant jelly gives this dish the sweetness that will make it more palatable to those who are not venison fans...yet.

VENISON LOAF

Ingredients

2 (8-count) pkgs. crescent rolls

1 lb. ground venison

1 lb. ground pork or turkey sausage

1 medium onion, chopped

1 (24 oz.) jar spaghetti sauce

1 (16 oz.) container small-curd
   cottage cheese

1 egg

½ cup grated Parmesan cheese

16 oz. shredded mozzarella cheese

½ cup milk

¼ cup sesame seeds

Directions

Preheat the oven to 350°.

In a 9 x 13-inch pan, stretch out the contents from one package of crescent rolls, forming a solid rectangle of dough.

Brown the ground venison, sausage, and onion. Drain off fat. Add spaghetti sauce and stir.

In another bowl, mix cottage cheese, egg, and Parmesan cheese.

Now in the pan, layer the ingredients as follows:

   ½ of meat mixture

   cottage cheese mixture

   ½ of mozzarella cheese

   remaining meat mixture

   remaining mozzarella cheese

Unfold the contents from the second package of crescent rolls and stretch out to form one rectangle. Lay it on top of the meat and cheese mixture. Seal the edges of dough together. Brush a little milk on top of crust and sprinkle on sesame seeds.

Bake for 45 minutes. Let cool for 15 minutes before serving.

Tip: Serve with Evelyn's Potato Salad (page 154).

EASY VENISON MEAT LOAF

Ingredients

1 lb. ground venison

1 lb. hamburger

2 eggs

¼ cup ketchup

½ tsp. seasoned salt

1 tsp. curry powder

Directions

Preheat oven to 375°. Mix together all ingredients and form into a loaf.

Bake for 30 minutes or until done.

Tip: This tasty and easy main dish is great for teaching young children or grandchildren to cook. Watch their faces as they announce to the family that they made supper!

EASY AND HEARTY VENISON SAUSAGE CHOWDER

Ingredients

1 lb. ground venison sausage

1 (15 oz.) can cream-style corn

1 (15 oz.) can potato soup

Directions

Brown sausage in a skillet, drain, and put into a Crock-Pot. Pour the creamed corn and potato soup into the Crock-Pot and stir.

Turn Crock-Pot to low setting and cook for 6 to 8 hours or turn to high for shorter cooking time of 3 to 4 hours.

OLD TIMER MOUNTAINEER HASH

Ingredients

1 medium onion, chopped

1 medium green pepper, chopped

3 T. butter

1 lb. ground venison

2 cups canned tomatoes, undrained
   and chopped

1 tsp. chili powder

¼ tsp. pepper

½ cup uncooked rice

1 tsp. salt

Directions

Preheat oven to 350°. Cook onion and pepper in butter until the onion is yellow. Add ground venison and cook until mixture falls apart. Drain fat.

Add tomatoes, chili powder, pepper, rice, and salt. Mix and pour into greased baking dish. Cover.

Bake for 45 minutes.

VENISON AND BEEF MEAT LOAF

Ingredients

1 medium onion, diced

1 or 2 garlic cloves, crushed

½ lb. bacon, chopped

1 lb. ground venison

1 lb. ground hamburger

1 egg

1 (2 oz.) packet onion soup mix

½ cup oats

Salt

Pepper

Topping

1 cup ketchup

2 T. Worcestershire sauce

2 T. mustard (or honey mustard)

Directions

Preheat oven to 375°.

Sauté onion, garlic, and bacon in a skillet. (The bacon doesn't have to fully cook because it will be baked.) Drain grease, remove from skillet, and allow mixture to cool.

Place ground venison and ground beef in a large bowl. Add egg, onion soup mix, and oats. Add bacon mixture and combine. Put into loaf pan. Salt and pepper the top.

Topping

Combine ketchup, Worcestershire sauce, mustard. Spread on top of meat loaf.

Bake for 45 minutes.

FAVORITE VENISON MEAT LOAF

Ingredients

2 eggs

1½ lbs. ground venison

1 (8 oz.) can tomato sauce

½ cup breadcrumbs

½ cup chopped onion

¼ cup chopped green pepper

1 tsp. salt

1 tsp. pepper

Dash dried thyme

Dash dried marjoram

Directions

Beat the eggs together. Add remaining ingredients, mixing well. Put in loaf pan.

Bake at 350° for 1 hour 15 minutes.

THE HIGH COST OF FREE MEAT

Chuck and Kathy Bentley and their children moved into the house across the field from us in the late 1990s. During our first conversation as new neighbors, Chuck and I (Steve) discovered we did similar work—we were musicians. Chuck had just finished recording a CD, and he gave us a copy. The production was wonderful. Because our very talented son had gone to college leaving us without an in-house producer, we asked Chuck for his producer's name and contact information. The name he gave us was Lindsey Williams.

Proving that it really can be a small world, nearly a decade earlier Lindsey had given our son, Nathan, guitar lessons. Knowing Lindsey's production and instrumental skills, as well as his cordial demeanor, we connected with him and promptly got started recording a new CD. During the recording of "This House Still Stands," Lindsey and I discovered our mutual interest in hunting. We managed to not let our talk about guns and chasing critters interfere with recording music, but it wasn't easy.

As they say, "The rest is hysterical." It was comical how quickly we bonded over hunting. We couldn't wait for deer season to start! Finally opening day arrived. I was especially excited about including Lindsey in my hunting plans because I'd found out he'd not yet bagged a whitetail. There's hardly anything that gives a veteran hunter more satisfaction than helping a first timer experience the thrill of success. When it finally happened, I'm not sure which of us felt more elation.

While we've since had many great moments of triumph in the woods together, including the downing of "Doezilla" (Lindsey's eye-popping 150-pound Tennessee doe) and our unforgettable "double doe" morning, his first deer remains one of our all-time favorite memories. But we're not the only ones who took special note of Lindsey's first deer. His wife, Susan, noticed it too. In fact, there were details of her hubby's exploit that probably would have gone unmentioned had she not documented them in her blog. With her permission, we share her well-written account of Lindsey's hunt.

THERE'S ONE BORN EVERY MINUTE

BY SUSAN WILLIAMS

No, I am not referring to a spike in the deer population. I reference, of course, that famous quote by P.T. Barnum, the great American showman, businessman, and scam artist, of the Ringling Brothers, Barnum and Bailey Circus fame. Barnum is the oft-quoted source of the famous phrase: "There's a sucker born every minute."

But since you're reading this story, I am going to take a wild guess and speculate that I might not be the only sucker in these here parts. There might be a few more of you out there who, just as I did, bought into the "Big Lie."

To what big lie do I refer, you ask? This sucker, er, innocent, bought into the idea her husband cleverly used to sell her on hunting. Not that he would *purposefully* try to manipulate me, but here's how it went down.

One day I was in the kitchen, minding my own business, cooking something that was doubtless both delicious and economical for dinner because, after all, I'm a pretty good cook. But even more importantly, I know we aren't made out of money, so part of my job as chief cook and bottle washer is to watch for sales at the grocery store and keep our food costs down.

Meat is so expensive. In fact, we hardly ever ate red meat due to the expense and my frugality and desire to live within our hard-earned means (she said as she polished up her halo and batted her eyelashes virtuously).

So one day my sweet husband, Lindsey, cozies up to me in the kitchen.

Him: "Mmm. That smells good. Whatcha makin'?"

Me: "Oh…just a roast chicken."

Him: "Mmm. That'll be great. Hey, hon, you know…I've been thinking…"

Me: "Mm hmm…" I was concentrating on sprinkling spices on the delicious (and cheap!) chicken.

Him: "You know, Steve mentioned the other day that he'd be happy to take me hunting with him. And it occurred to me that hunting might be a really good hobby for me to take up. Because, after all, there's *free meat!*"

Me: "Hmm…" So I'm standing there thinking, "Free meat? Free meat sounds good. And our friend Steve is an expert hunter. He could really teach my man how to be a successful hunter. And then we'd have all that *free meat.* Think of the *savings* on our food bills through the year."

Me: "Well, okay, I guess. That might be good."

Yup. That's about how it went down. And let me tell you, if there really is one born every minute, that was my minute. Because here's how all that *free meat* happened that year:

Hunting license: $135

Gun: $175

Ammo: $50

Camo clothes: $50

Boots: $80

And these are very conservative estimates! And lest we forget, where were we going to store all that *free meat*? We purchased a freezer: $500 (honestly, I'm grateful for it, but still…).

And then there were the "processing fees" once the *free meat* had been procured: $75.

That first year alone, my husband shot a $1,000 deer. And I thought I was the trophy wife. Harrumph! And now each year there are guns, gadgets, and gewgaws that must be added to supplement the arsenal:

Bow: $400 to $800

Arrows: $55

Other guns: $350

Rain gear: $65

Blind: $400

Special shower soap: $5.50

Special laundry soap: $6.75

Animal calls: $40 to $50

Decoys of various species: $ (who even knows?)

In the interest of being charitable, I am not even going to mention that little trip across the continent to hunt elk in Colorado.

Now you might think I'm ungrateful for all the wonderful, delicious game we eat each year. And if you think that, you'd be wrong. I have learned how to cook it, and cook it deliciously. I'm grateful for the health benefits that come from eating meat that is truly free range and low in fat. I'm grateful for the joy it brings my husband when he comes home from a day in the woods enjoying God's beautiful creation. I'm grateful for the camaraderie he shares with Steve, who has become not only a mentor but a true brother.

I'm thankful that their friendship has bonded our family closer to Annie, and to their wonderful children, and grandchildren. Blessing after blessing has come into our lives because I encouraged my dear husband that day to follow his bliss, to pursue a hobby that brings him joy and satisfaction. If I were asked the question all over again, I'd respond the same way. It's been totally worth it. But *free meat*? Not so much!

SUSAN'S VENISON MEATBALLS

Ingredients

¼ cup pine nuts, toasted

3 cups 1-inch cubed day-old Italian bread

2 lbs. ground venison

3 eggs, beaten

3 garlic cloves, minced

¾ cup grated Pecorino Romano cheese (or Parmesan cheese)

¼ cup loosely packed Italian flat-leaf parsley, finely chopped

½ tsp. + 1 tsp. salt (coarse-grain sea salt preferred), divided

½ tsp. freshly ground black pepper

1 (16 oz.) pkg. spaghetti noodles

1½ cups tomato sauce

½ cup grated Parmigiano Reggiano (Parmesan cheese)

Directions

Preheat oven to 375°.

Toast the pine nuts by sautéing them for two minutes until lightly brown.

In a shallow bowl, soak the bread cubes in a cup of water for 1 to 2 minutes. (Use the best quality bread possible so it has a little oomph and won't turn to mush.) Drain the bread cubes and squeeze with your fingers to press out excess moisture.

In a large bowl, combine the bread cubes, venison, eggs, garlic, Pecorino Romano, parsley, pine nuts, ½ teaspoon salt, and pepper. Mix with your hands.

With wet hands, form meatballs to the size of golf balls. (If desired, you can use an ice cream scoop to form the meatballs.) Make sure they are uniform in size. Place them on a cookie sheet or in a greased mini muffin tin.

Bake for 15 to 20 minutes until nicely brown.

Bring 6 quarts of water to boil in a large pot and add 1 teaspoon salt. Add spaghetti, cook according to package instructions, and drain.

In a 10- or 12-inch sauté pan, combine tomato sauce and meatballs. Heat until meatballs are hot all the way through.

Put the pasta into the sauté pan with the meatballs and toss gently to mix.

Divide onto plates and sprinkle with Parmigiano Reggiano.

VENISON SAUSAGE BREAKFAST BURRITO

Ingredients

1 lb. venison sausage

1 small onion, chopped

12 eggs

½ cup water

1 can green chilies

8 flour tortillas

Nonstick cooking spray

1 cup shredded cheddar cheese

½ cup sour cream

½ cup Quick and Easy Salsa (page 148)

Directions

Brown venison sausage and onion. Drain fat.

Beat eggs and combine with water. Stir in green chilies. Pour into sausage and onion mixture.

Cook until eggs have no liquid remaining, being careful not to overcook.

Spray a flat skillet with oil and heat tortillas until they turn light brown.

Fill each tortilla with scrambled egg mixture. Top with cheese, sour cream, and Quick and Easy Salsa.

SWEET AND SALTY CROCK-POT VENISON

Ingredients

Venison roast

Salt

Pepper

Tony's Cajun Seasoning

1 (32 oz.) can beef broth

2 beef bouillon cubes, mixed with
    2 cups hot water

1 cup cooking wine or sherry (wine's
    acidic quality tenderizes meat) or
    1 cup beef broth

1 (18 oz.) jar red currant jelly

1 large red onion, sliced

2 T. cornstarch (plus 4 T. cold water)

2 cups sliced carrots, cut on the
    diagonal

8 oz. mushrooms

4 large potatoes, cubed

Directions

Rinse venison roast in cold water and pat dry. Rub with ample amounts of salt, pepper, and Tony's Cajun Seasoning. Set aside.

In a large Crock-Pot, pour beef broth, beef bouillon with water, cooking wine, and red currant jelly. Stir until everything is mixed well. Add venison and onion.

Cook on medium high heat all day.

Two or three hours before serving, mix cornstarch in water and whisk, dissolving lumps. Mix into Crock-Pot contents to thicken to a terrific gravy consistency. Add carrots, mushrooms, and potatoes, and continue to cook.

VENISON QUESADILLAS

Ingredients

Marinade
2 T. lime juice or the juice of 2 limes
1 tsp. cumin
1 garlic clove, crushed
Dash salt
2 T. Worcestershire sauce

Quesadillas
Venison, thinly sliced and marinated
2 T. olive oil
1 onion, diced
3 bell peppers (green, red, and/or yellow), sliced
Flour tortillas, large
Cheddar or other cheese, shredded
Butter
Optional: cilantro, tomatoes, black beans, corn, other vegetables
Optional toppings: Quick and Easy Salsa (page 148), sour cream, Fruit Chipotle Chutney (page 161)

Directions

Combine marinade ingredients in a ziplock plastic bag. Add thinly sliced venison and refrigerate for at least 30 minutes. Remove meat from marinade and sauté in olive oil until done. Set meat aside.

Sauté onion and peppers to desired tenderness. Set aside.

On one half of a flour tortilla, place cheese, meat, and vegetable mixture. Add cilantro, tomatoes, black beans, corn, and any other desired vegetables. Fold the tortilla in half and place on an amply buttered grill or skillet. Heat until the quesadilla is warm throughout and golden brown on the outside.

Serve with Quick and Easy Salsa, sour cream, or Fruit Chipotle Chutney.

PAN-FRIED VENISON

Ingredients

1 cup all-purpose flour
1 tsp. salt
½ tsp. black pepper
½ tsp. garlic powder
2 T. olive oil
2 T. butter
Venison, cubed

Directions

Mix flour, salt, black pepper, garlic powder (and other spices as desired) in a large ziplock bag.

Place venison, a few cubes at a time, into the plastic bag, dredging them in the flour mixture. Remove and set aside.

Melt olive oil and butter in a skillet. Turn burner to medium heat, and fry venison until the desired doneness. (Fully cooked with a crunchy, golden-brown crust tastes great.)

Tip: Serve with delicious Sweet-and-Sour Sauce (page 193).

GRILLED VENISON TENDERLOINS

Ingredients

Annie's Favorite Marinade (page 187)

Venison tenderloins or steaks

Directions

Marinate steaks for 12 to 24 hours in a large ziplock bag stored in the refrigerator.

Put the steaks on the grate over hot coals. Cook approximately 2 minutes on each side, turning only once.

If you're in the woods, wait until there is no flame left in the campfire. Put the steaks on forked sticks and hang the meat 4 inches or so above the coals. Cook 2 minutes each side, turning as needed until well done. Hickory or apple wood is great for grilling steaks.

DELICIOUS TENDERLOIN BACKSTRAP

Ingredients

Venison Marinade (page 189)

Venison tenderloin (backstrap)

Salt

Pepper

Garlic powder

Tony's Creole Seasoning

Onions, thinly sliced

Mushrooms, sliced

Kitchen string

Steak sauce

Bacon strips

Directions

Marinate meat in Venison Marinade. Remove meat from marinade, rinse in cold water, and pat dry.

Butterfly the tenderloin backstrap, almost cutting it in half. Salt and pepper the inside of the meat. Add garlic powder and Tony's Creole Seasoning. Now lay a bed of onions and mushrooms on top of the seasonings and meat.

Soak kitchen string in water until thoroughly wet, bring the "halves" of meat together, and tie with string. Sprinkle salt, pepper, and garlic powder on the outside, along with any other seasonings if desired.

Cover the meat with your favorite steak sauce and let marinate for a couple of hours.

Wrap the tenderloin in strips of bacon and secure with toothpicks. Place the meat on a hot grill over indirect heat and cook until desired doneness. Enjoy!

Tip: Butterfly a chop by cutting it down the middle, leaving about one inch at the bottom. Fold the chop over on the cutting board, creating a nice thick steak.

VENISON STEAK AND GRAVY

SUBMITTED BY EVELYN BLEDSOE

Ingredients

1 T. shortening

8 venison steaks

1 cup + 4 T. all-purpose flour

Salt

Pepper

3 beef bouillon cubes

Directions

Heat the shortening in an electric skillet or a large iron skillet.

Tenderize steaks with a mallet or small saucer by pounding until the meat is pulverized and tendons are broken up.

Dredge the meat in 1 cup of flour and put in skillet. Brown the steaks on both sides. Sprinkle with salt and pepper after turning.

Mix the beef cubes with water per package instructions and pour into skillet. Cook slowly until the steaks are done, 2 to 3 hours. Keep adding water as needed to keep meat from drying out. (The broth should come up about halfway on the meat.)

Put 4 T. of flour in a small jar and add 1 cup of cold water. Shake well to blend. Pour flour mixture into the skillet and stir until blended for a gravy. Let the steak and gravy simmer for 15 minutes, stirring often—even whisking with a wire utensil—to eliminate lumps.

Tip: Serve hot with mashed potatoes and green beans—and don't forget the Sylvie Biscuits (page 163).

VENISON HOT DOG CROWD PLEASER

SUBMITTED BY EVELYN BLEDSOE

Ingredients

4 cups water

3 (28 oz.) cans tomato puree (or
  canned tomatoes or tomato sauce)

10 lbs. ground venison

10 beef bouillon cubes

1 T. sugar

1 T. red pepper flakes

1 large onion, chopped

2 T. garlic powder

2 T. chili powder

1 T. celery seed

1 T. basil

1 T. oregano

1½ T. cumin

½ T. sage

4 dozen hot dogs

4 dozen hot dog buns

Directions

Put water and tomato puree into a heavy, 10-quart kettle.

Brown the ground venison a little bit at a time in an iron skillet. Drain the grease, and use paper towels to soak up any additional grease. As the burger browns, add it to the kettle mixture.

When all the burger is in the kettle, cook over medium heat, stirring well. Add beef cubes, sugar, red pepper flakes, and onion. Cover the kettle and bring to a boil. Lower the heat, add all the spices, and cook slowly for approximately 2 hours or until the meat is tender. Stir often as it cooks. Keep skimming off as much grease as possible. Add more water as needed.

After the mixture has cooked 1½ hours, taste to determine if you want to add more of any spice.

Serve sauce by pouring over cooked hot dogs or hot dogs and buns.

SLOPPY JOES

Ingredients

4 lbs. venison burger

2 large onions, chopped

2 large green bell peppers, chopped

1 (40 oz.) bottle ketchup

2 T. chili powder

12 hamburger buns

Directions

Mix all ingredients in skillet, except buns. Cook and stir 1 hour or until done. Add more ketchup if needed for desired thickness.

Serve on or over hamburger buns.

Tip: Coleslaw (page 148) goes great with Sloppy Joes!

HEARTY SAUSAGE AND BEANS

Ingredients

1 (15 oz.) can white kidney (cannellini) beans

2 (15 oz.) cans red kidney beans

1 lb. cooked venison sausage, cut into 1-inch pieces

2 large onions, chopped

2 large sweet red peppers, chopped

1 large green bell pepper, chopped

¼ cup brown sugar, packed

2 T. steak sauce

1 T. cider vinegar

1 tsp. Worcestershire sauce

Directions

Rinse all beans, drain, and set aside.

In a large skillet, cook sausage for 2 to 3 minutes. Stir in onion and bell pepper. Cook and stir until sausage is lightly browned and vegetables are tender. Drain.

In a separate bowl, combine brown sugar, steak sauce, cider vinegar, and Worcestershire sauce. Stir the mixture into the skillet of meat and vegetables. Add the beans. Cook and stir until heated through.

CHRISTIAN'S FIRST DEER

RELATED BY CHRISTIAN'S DAD, CURT CHRISTMAN

October 16 started cool and somewhat cloudy in our neck of the New York woods. I sat with Christian for his first hunt while his brother, Corwin, bow-hunted a few hundred yards away. Christian and I were hoping to intercept deer coming off the hayfield to our left.

The morning hunt yielded nothing, so we headed home around nine thirty for a short rest and breakfast. The warm fire in the woodstove begged us to stay, but I knew if we stayed too long we would succumb to the desire to close our eyes, thus only dreaming of downing the *big* one. Christian decided he needed warmer clothes, so we headed out. We stopped for some snacks and fuel for our gas-guzzling pickup and then hurried to the co-op to shop for hunting clothes.

A hefty $148 later (out of Christian's pocket), we were off to our afternoon hunt. We moved from our earlier location, and set up in front of some small cedars. After forty-five minutes or so, I was feeling drowsy. I told Christian that since he'd spent much of the morning watching the insides of his eyelids while I kept watch for brown furry things, it was his turn to stand watch. I'd only "doesed" for around ten minutes when I was awoken by the loud kaboom of a muzzleloader. I estimated the distance at 500 yards away. I jumped up and grabbed my gun. Christian was already at full alert as he looked for fleeing deer.

A few seconds later I saw Christian shoulder his gun. A mature doe came to a halt right in front of our position. As she stood broadside and looked back in the direction from which she'd come, I heard Christian's muzzleloader deliver its load. What happened next is something I've enjoyed remembering since that unforgettable day.

As the smoke cleared, I watched Christian's eyes display the thrill of connecting with a big game animal. But then my heart sank as I saw doubt spread across his face as the doe sped away. Drawing from twenty-seven years of deer hunting experience, I knew the deer had been hit. Her high kick and

labored-but-hurried departure was proof enough. But Christian didn't know what I knew. Hoping to relieve him of a little bit of his worry, I forced calmness into my voice and said, "Son, quietly reload. After a few minutes, we'll look for the blood trail to follow."

When we walked over to the place of bullet impact, a mere thirty-one yards away, I looked for the telltale signs that the deer had been wounded. I didn't find any blood or hair. I could see where the dirt had been dug up as she made her escape, but there was hardly any other sign to be found. We tracked as best we could without the advantage of snow or mud. We stopped a short fifty yards later when all indications of a deer on the run were gone. We had no clue which direction she'd gone.

I cautiously wandered over to the edge of the woods where I suspect she'd headed. I stood there a minute or so looking hard for just one more sign of a fast-moving deer. With nothing visible, I made one of the hardest decisions for a hunter—to stop the search and wait. I instructed Christian that if a wounded animal is allowed to lie down and lick its wounds, the chances of finding it are better. Though it was painful for him, he agreed to wait.

I silently whispered a prayer as we settled down, telling the Lord that for Christian's sake we needed some sign that the fleeing doe was hit. In the next instant I could hardly believe what I saw. As I lay my muzzleloader down in the grass at the edge of the woods, I spotted a small but distinct puddle of clear slime. I touched it with my gloved finger and lifted it to my nose. I detected the sour smell of stomach acid. I told Christian to take courage—that his first trophy was definitely hit. If we did the search right, there was a good chance of retrieving her.

At four thirty we were ready to make our move. I wanted Christian to circle the patch of woods I was about to enter in case I spooked the deer. That way he might have a chance to intercept it on the other side. However, he wanted to be with me if the deer was found, so I gave in. It paid off to stick together because after walking fifty yards, I saw a patch of white fur. As I carefully studied the sight, I could see the snow-white patch was surrounded by grayish brown fur.

I pointed out the doe to my son, and we vigorously gave each other a celebratory handshake and hug. As we started toward the deer, Christian couldn't keep from running ahead to his downed trophy. It was joy beyond measure to see him lean over the doe and then grin ear to ear. We called Corwin on our radio to give him the news. He left his treestand to join us. We later learned that his premature departure spooked a deer as he descended. Oh well!

Christian did a fine job field dressing the 135-pound doe. I walked ahead of my sons as they worked together to drag the prize to the edge of the field and our rig. Christian called his mom on his cell, so when we got home she met us in the driveway with a big smile and a camera, ready for taking photos that will be treasured for years to come.

How glad we all were that we didn't let the sleepy bug bite us when we got back to the warm fire that morning. We learned an important lesson about how determination can yield exciting moments, long-lasting memories, and the main ingredient in one of our favorite venison meals we affectionately call "Venzen Sloppy Joes."

VENZEN SLOPPY JOES

Ingredients

1 lb. ground venison

1 small onion, chopped

⅓ cup red wine or cider vinegar

⅓ cup ketchup

2 T. mustard

1 tsp. salt

½ tsp. pepper

1 tsp. garlic powder

1 cup brown sugar (or maple syrup)

4 hamburger buns

1 cup shredded cheddar cheese

Directions

Quickly brown the venison and onion. As soon as the red is gone from the meat, add the red wine, ketchup, and mustard. While stirring, add salt, pepper, and garlic powder. Cook for a short time and then slowly stir in the brown sugar. Let cook for at least 15 minutes on low heat.

Layer bread and sloppy joe mixture in a bowl, top with cheddar cheese, and serve.

Tip: Adding tomatoes to meat naturally tenderizes it because the acid in the tomatoes helps break down the fiber of the meat. Tomatoes also help cover any gamy taste.

VENISON STEAKS

Ingredients

1½ to 2 lbs. venison steaks

1 cup buttermilk

1 cup water

Marinade

2 cloves garlic, minced

3 T. butter, melted

1 tsp. hot sauce

2 T. red wine

2 T. freshly chopped rosemary

1 sprig thyme, leaves stemmed and
  freshly chopped

1 tsp. paprika

1 tsp. dried basil

½ tsp. salt

1 tsp. black pepper

¼ tsp. cayenne pepper

1 T. honey

Steak Preparation

½ cup olive oil

Tin foil

Directions

The night before, prepare the meat by soaking it in equal parts buttermilk and water. The next morning, pour off the liquid and place the meat in a large bowl or ziplock bag.

Mix the marinade ingredients and pour over the meat. Cover and refrigerate for 4 hours.

Remove meat from marinade and allow to sit at room temperature for 20 to 30 minutes. Pat steaks dry and coat with olive oil.

Place steaks on a hot grill for 4 to 7 minutes per side. (The time depends on the grill, the thickness of the steaks, and how you prefer them cooked.) When steaks are done, put them on a plate, cover with tin foil, let set for 5 to 10 minutes, and then serve.

Tip: This recipe also works well for a 2-pound venison roast.

THE ONE THAT ALMOST GOT AWAY

AS TOLD BY CURT CHRISTMAN

If anyone ever deserved to achieve the taking of his or her first deer, it was my son Corwin. From the time he could barely pull up his own boots, I took him hunting with me. All my children went with me from time to time, often on afternoon hunts but rarely in the early morning hours. Corwin, on the other hand, crawled out of his warm, cozy bed morning after morning. His determination to see me take a deer was stronger than any I've ever seen in a child. At times it seemed almost stronger than my own!

For the previous two years, Corwin had hunted with archery equipment because, in the state of New York, a hunter must be sixteen to use a firearm. So Corwin and I toted our bows and arrows many a sleepy morning in hopes of getting close to the elusive whitetail. On this day, as hard as we tried, we were nearing the end of a fruitless season. We had spent many days without seeing any deer, so we were tempted to pack it in. However, our die-hard attitudes prevailed. Once again, we crunched our way through the frozen grass and hauled our tired bodies into our deer stands.

After making sure Corwin was safe in his stand and settling his brother, Christian, in his, I went to mine. As I settled in on that Tuesday morning, I sighed deeply and offered up a prayer. I rarely pray to take a deer, but desperate times bring desperate measures. I said, "Lord, as much as I would like to get my own deer, I want Corwin and Christian to be successful." We had put a lot of money and hours into the trip, and coming home empty-handed would not be a good thing.

Looking around the cold, damp woods, I resolved to the likelihood that I'd have a long wait. Around a quarter after seven, I heard that telltale sound of large-bodied animals moving through the brush. I spotted movement in the goldenrods about 100 yards out. Two deer were hurrying by, passing in front of me but behind too much brush for a decent shot. The excitement of actually seeing deer kept me content for a while, but boredom and the pressure of going home empty-handed got me thinking of ways to create some action. I called Christian on the cell phone and told him to get ready to put on a drive for Corwin and me. I moved to another fixed stand that a friend had built just off the road overlooking a gas well. Just as I got up on the stand, I spotted Corwin about 250 yards away wildly waving to me to meet him up the hill.

I waited for Christian to finish out the drive and then descended to the ground to join him to look for Corwin. We found him standing hopeful and excited on a gas well road. He said he had hit a small doe and had seen good blood. To me "good blood" means a lot of it, but to Corwin's inexperienced eyes any red liquid was sufficient. We located the four or five drops of blood Corwin had found and then searched for any other sign, but there was none.

I quizzed Corwin a couple of times on the deer's action after he'd taken the shot. He described how it seemed to trot off a little "humped," which, to me, was a clue that he had gut shot the doe. With that, the three of us spread out and began our search through the goldenrod and barren apple trees. Christian followed a wide path, and a few minutes later I heard him yell that he'd found the arrow. I hopefully asked if it was stuck in a deer, but his reply was negative. My hopes were dashed.

We inspected the arrow first by sight. There was good, clear blood from tip to fletching, a sign that Corwin had managed a complete pass through. On the tip there was white hair and some fat, not a good sign because the belly hair of a deer is white. Then I put my nose to the arrow as a test and didn't like what I found: the sour, rank smell of gut. Not good. From one end to the other, the arrow had the dreaded smell of the inside of a deer's food-burning machine. Not a pleasant odor to say the least. Now I knew we were dealing with a deer that could suffer for a few days before dying. Not good. The problem was that we didn't have a lot of time for tracking.

After searching for an hour or so, we gave up and moved on—disappointed in not getting the meat and for leaving an animal in distress. It's hard for me to lose my own deer but much harder to watch my son feeling the pain of his moment of triumph turning into disaster. Finally, with a ton of reluctance, we headed back to where we were staying. On the way, we stopped to drown our sorrows with some hot food and the warm atmosphere of a little diner nationally famous for its hot dogs. It helped a little, but the sting of the lost deer didn't go away.

Wednesday morning proved to be too cold for sitting in a treestand. We slept in and packed our gear in our vehicle for the trip home. I couldn't get Corwin's deer off my mind, and I felt the need to relieve our hurting hearts by one more search. I knew there was a chance the wounded deer had survived the cold night. Deer will often go downhill to a water source to wait and heal up, and that was an area we hadn't completely searched. So we headed back to the woods.

I set Christian up on watch in case we flushed out a buck during our search. As Corwin and I trudged the creek bottom, I knew that looking for the doe was like looking for a dime in a football stadium filled with people. We gave it a good try, but with no results we left the creek bottom. As we headed uphill, I looked up toward our last slim chance. Above us was a plantation of thick, nearly impassable evergreen trees. A deer could hide in there for weeks and we would never find it. I instructed Corwin to crawl through, if needed, as this was our last hope of finding his wounded deer. I tried several times to penetrate the thick brush in the woods and had to resort to crawling in. Only if I bent completely over could I make my way through parts of it. From my knees I could look down between the rows, but I couldn't see or hear Corwin.

As I approached the top half of the woods, I set my mind to face Corwin's disappointment once again. I felt the slap and scratch of branches on my face and body. All at once one of the sweetest sounds a hunter-dad could ever hear reached my thankful ears.

"I found my deer, Daddy!" Corwin's excited voice came rolling through the mass of scraggly branches. "I'm coming, Corwin!" I yelled back.

I found myself not caring at all about the sharp branches that tore at me. Ahead lay the prize we so longed to see. I had to stop a few times to get a bead on Corwin's location. At last there he was with a grin as big as my own twenty-eight years earlier when I'd dropped my first deer.

Corwin's deer was a yearling, a perfect, tender, table-meat doe that any young bow hunter could be proud of. We all agreed that the next morning, after a good night's sleep, we would honor the life of the animal by enjoying one of our favorite dishes that venison can yield: a simple and easy breakfast of fried backstrap and eggs.

Corwin easily dragged his young prize up the hill to the road. Rites of passage come in many forms, and in our family one rite is field dressing the first deer, with some help from Dad, of course. Corwin did a great job.

Our ride home was an exercise in telling, retelling, and telling again the story of the one that almost got away. The sweetest part was that after many years of watching and wishing, Corwin at last added his name to the elite list of hunters who have taken a deer with a bow and arrow.

CURT'S HEALTHY BREAKFAST BACKSTRAPS

Ingredients

½ venison backstrap
   (approximately 7 inches)
¼ stick butter
1 large onion, chopped
3 to 4 large cloves garlic, minced

Directions

Slice the backstrap into ¼-inch strips.

In a skillet, melt the butter and add the venison. Cook on medium to high heat. Add the onion and garlic. Cook until the red no longer shows in the center of meat. (Be careful not to overcook.)

Tip: Serve with eggs and toast. With a quick, simple breakfast, timing is everything. Be sure you start with the meat about 1½ minutes before you put the bread in the toaster and start the eggs. With that plan, everything should be done at the same time.

Tip: To avoid fighting over the tasty backstrap, the first and last piece should always go to the one who took the shot and provided the venison.

"ON THE RUN" BACKSTRAPS

BY DAVE QUICK

Ingredients

2 lbs. venison backstrap

Italian vinegar and oil salad dressing
(or marinade)

Salt

Directions

This recipe is super simple and great for folks like us—grandparents of nine grandkids and always on the go. Using a good-size venison backstrap, cut sections about 3 inches thick. Trim so all you have is nice red meat. Then treat like you would butterfly chops, by cutting down the middle, leaving about 1 inch at the bottom. Fold your "chop" over on the cutting board, creating a thick steak.

Pound the steaks with a meat hammer to tenderize. I find this works very well with larger or older deer.

Place your steaks in a large ziplock bag, keeping them separated as much as possible even as they lie nice and flat in the bag. Pour in the Italian dressing and perhaps a teaspoon or so of salt. Be sure the dressing is on both sides of the meat in the bag. Now, lay the bag flat on the counter and squeeze out the air as you carefully zip the bag closed. Fold the bag up until you have a nice, compact package. Place in the fridge overnight.

When ready to cook, start a charcoal fire and allow it to get glowing-red hot. However, moderation is the key here. Do not use too much charcoal. You will close the vents on the grill once the meat is on to reduce the heat. Sear the meat at first, but after that only turn the meat once. Watch the temperature, keeping it modest. Be careful not to overcook the steaks. They should have just a hint of pink in the center when done.

Serve with green beans and mashed potatoes. This is superfast and easy when you're in a hurry yet still want a tasty and convenient meal.

GRANDPA'S VENISON BACKSTRAP

Ingredients

1½ cups saltine crackers

3 eggs

½ cup milk

1 tsp. salt

Pepper (or McCormick's Seasoning Salt)

1 venison backstrap

½ cup vegetable oil

Directions

In a flat dish, crush the crackers.

In a bowl, whisk the eggs, milk, salt, and pepper.

Cut the venison backstrap into butterfly chops, approximately ¼-inch thick on each half. Cover each butterfly chop in the cracker crumbs and dredge in the egg mixture. Cover again with cracker crumbs and place on a large dish.

Once ready, place backstrap in a large skillet with vegetable oil. Cook 3 minutes or so per side over medium heat until desired doneness.

VENISON ROAST WITH SOUP

Ingredients

3 to 4 lbs. venison roast

Seasoning salt

1 (10.5 oz.) can cream of
  mushroom soup

1 (10.5 oz.) can cream of celery soup

1 (32 oz.) container beef broth

1 medium onion, chopped
  (or 2 T. onion flakes)

2 to 4 medium-size carrots

2 to 4 medium potatoes

2 cups water

Directions

Rub the roast with seasoning salt and place in a baking pan with a lid. Spoon in cream of mushroom and cream of celery soups. Add beef broth and onion.

Cut carrots and potatoes into bite-size pieces and add to pan. Add water and mix everything well.

Cover pan and bake at 325° for 3 hours.

Serve the soup, carrots, and potatoes in a bowl and the meat on a plate. (The soup has a wonderful consistency, and the soup and meat taste great!)

VENISON TENDERLOIN CELEBRATION

Ingredients

2 venison tenderloins

1 stick butter or margarine

2 cups sliced mushrooms

1 onion, diced or chopped (optional)

Salt, to taste

Directions

Cut the venison tenderloins into thin, bite-size strips.

In a wok or heavy skillet, heat the butter to a relatively high temperature. Place the tenderloins in the wok and brown, approximately 2 minutes. (Don't overcook or the meat will turn tough.)

Add the mushrooms to the wok. If desired, add onion and salt. Continue stirring for 2 minutes or so, turn off the heat. Cover the wok with the lid or foil and allow contents to steam for approximately 5 minutes.

VENISON BARBECUE STIR-FRY

Ingredients

2 venison steaks

1 cup barbecue sauce

½ T. vegetable oil

2 cups mixed stir-fry vegetables

1 (4 oz.) can cut mushrooms, undrained

1 cup uncooked instant rice

Directions

Cut venison steaks into stir-fry-size chunks. Marinate in the barbecue sauce for a few hours or coat the meat for immediate use.

Heat the wok or heavy skillet to cooking temperature and add vegetable oil. Quickly brown the venison, and then turn down the heat slightly. Add the stir-fry vegetables and mushrooms. If your wok has a dome lid, put the lid in place and allow to steam for 5 minutes.

Prepare the rice according to package instructions.

Serve the stir-fry over the cooked rice.

Tip: This is a great recipe for a fast-paced lifestyle. The barbecue sauce adds a delightful flavor.

SLICED VENISON ROAST WITH MUSHROOM GRAVY

Ingredients

1 (14.5 oz.) can cut green beans

1 (7.3 oz.) can cut mushrooms

1 lb. venison roast

3 strips bacon

1 (10.5 oz.) can cream of mushroom soup

8 oz. milk

1 cup flour

Directions

Cook the green beans. Drain the green beans while being sure to save the liquid.

Drain and save the liquid from the mushrooms.

Using a liquid injector, inject the liquid from the green beans and mushrooms into the roast. Wrap the roast with three strips of bacon and secure with toothpicks. Place roast in a roasting pan.

Cook at 300° for approximately 2 hours, until the center temperature is 170°.

Take the roaster out of the oven and pour the green beans into the liquid in the bottom of the roaster. Let the roast and green beans rest.

In a saucepan, mix the cream of mushroom soup with the milk. Stir in the mushrooms. Add the flour and mix well. Heat until thick and hot.

Cut the roast into thin slices on the bias. Ladle the gravy over the meat and serve.

Tip: Serve with Half Runner Green Beans (page 147) and Fireplace Baked Potatoes (page 153).

QUICK FAMILY VENISON STEW

Ingredients

1 lb. venison

4 medium potatoes, cut into pieces

3 medium onions, diced

4 to 6 large carrots, thinly sliced

3 ribs celery, thinly sliced

1 (32 oz.) container beef broth

4 T. ketchup

Directions

Cut the venison into bite-size chunks and place in a Crock-Pot. Add the potatoes, onions, carrots, and celery. Pour in the beef broth and enough water to cover everything. Add ketchup and mix everything well.

Let the stew simmer on medium for 6 to 8 hours.

Tip: This is an especially good recipe for tough cuts of meat, such as neck and shoulder.

 ## TIPS FOR CANNING VENISON OR ELK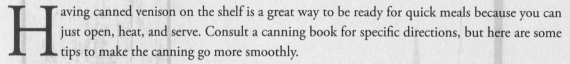

Having canned venison on the shelf is a great way to be ready for quick meals because you can just open, heat, and serve. Consult a canning book for specific directions, but here are some tips to make the canning go more smoothly.

- Cut venison into bite-size squares. Remove all fat and as much membrane as possible. (If you prefer, you can precook the meat prior to canning, which makes even quicker meal preparation possible. Consult your canning book for instructions.)

- According to canning directions, clean the desired number of pint or quart canning jars. (I recommend doing 4 to 5 quarts at a time.)

- Add one teaspoon of salt to each jar, followed by a small amount of boiling water. (I prefer to dissolve the salt this way before packing the meat.)

- Add venison to jars and top off with boiling water, leaving the amount of headspace recommended in canning directions.

- Process venison according to the canning directions for beef.

- Be sure to follow the specific directions that came with your pressure canner.

VENISON STEW FOR CANNING

Ingredients

2 quarts venison, canned

1 (32 oz.) container beef broth

2 (10.5 oz.) cans cream of celery soup

4 to 5 medium potatoes, chunked
   (w/skin or peeled)

2 medium onions, diced

6 T. ketchup

Salt

Directions

In a large pan with a lid, combine all ingredients. (You can add water to thicken or thin stew to the desired consistency.) Bring to a boil, and then reduce heat. Simmer for 2 to 3 hours until meat becomes tender. Remove from heat.

Wash and prepare canning jars. Have lids ready according to canning directions.

Add salt to the jars at the rate of ¼ teaspoon per pint (½ teaspoon per quart).

Ladle hot stew into jars, put on and adjust lids according to canning directions, and install rings. Place in pressure canner. Process quarts at 10 pounds for 1 hour 30 minutes or pints for 1 hour 15 minutes.

Remove jars and set on several layers of dish towels to cool. Inspect lids for tight seal. Label and store.

VENISON BARBECUE TENDERLOIN MEAL

Ingredients

2 venison tenderloins

4 T. ketchup

1½ T. barbecue sauce

2 baking potatoes

Vegetable of your choice

Directions

Take two venison tenderloins and place in covered pan, along with enough water to cover meat. Add ketchup and barbecue sauce.

Bring to boil and then reduce heat. Simmer for 2 to 3 hours or until the meat is "fall apart tender."

Bake or mash potatoes and prepare the vegetables.

Enjoy!

Tip: This recipe works well with other tender cuts of venison, such as backstrap cut into tenderloin-size strips or other rump or hindquarter cuts.

DAVE'S VENISON STROGANOFF

Ingredients

1 lb. venison tenderloin or steak,
    ½-inch thick

2 T. butter or margarine

½ lb. mushrooms, sliced

½ cup diced onion

1 (10.5 oz.) can condensed beef broth

2 T. ketchup

1 clove garlic, diced

1 T. salt

3 to 4 cups cooked noodles

3 T. flour

1 cup sour cream

Directions

Cut venison into ½-inch cubes.

Melt butter in skillet. Add mushrooms and onion, cooking and stirring until onion is tender. Remove from skillet.

In the same skillet, cook meat until light brown. Stir in beef broth, ketchup, garlic, and salt.

Cover and simmer for 15 minutes.

Prepare noodles per package instructions.

Blend flour into meat mixture. Add mushrooms and onion mixture. Heat to boiling, stirring constantly. Boil and stir 1 minute. Reduce heat. Add sour cream and continue stirring until well mixed. Serve over noodles.

VENISON RIGATONI

Ingredients

Rigatoni

1 (10.5 oz.) can cream of mushroom soup

1 quart jar of canned venison

Directions

In a large pan, boil the rigatoni. Drain.

In a separate pan, prepare cream of mushroom soup according to the directions.

Open jar of venison, drain, and rinse. Add the venison to the soup and let simmer.

That is all there is to it! Ladle the soup and venison over the rigatoni and serve piping hot, along with your choice of side dishes. This is a great recipe to use when you don't have much time to spend cooking.

VENISON D'PAPRIKA

Ingredients

2 to 2½ lbs. venison, 1-inch cubes

1½ cups flour

2 tsp. paprika, divided

Dash salt

Pinch pepper

3 to 4 T. oil

2 medium onions, chopped

2 to 3 cloves garlic, minced

1 tsp. marjoram (or Italian seasoning)

1 (29 oz.) can diced tomatoes

2 cups water

1 cup red wine (or beef broth)

1 cup sour cream (optional)

Directions

Roll venison cubes in flour seasoned with 1 teaspoon paprika, salt, and pepper.

Heat oil in heavy Dutch oven or cast-iron skillet. Over medium-high heat, brown cubes a few at a time. (If you crowd the pan with the cubes, they will steam instead of brown.) Remove to a warm dish after they've cooked.

After meat is browned, cook onion in same skillet over medium heat until browned. Add garlic, remaining paprika, marjoram, tomatoes, water, and wine.

Cover and simmer for 20 minutes.

Add browned meat, stir, and cook over low heat for 2 hours.

Just before serving, add sour cream if desired.

Tip: Serve over noodles, rice, or Texas toast.

UNCLE BOB'S VENISON LOAF

Ingredients

4 dashes Tabasco

⅓ cup V8 juice

1½ lbs. ground venison

⅓ cup applesauce

1 medium onion, diced

2 medium-large carrots, shredded

3 to 4 cloves garlic, crushed

Pinch of oregano

1 T. butter

Salt

Pepper

8 soda crackers, finely crushed

Directions

Mix Tabasco and V8 juice in a large mixing bowl. Add the venison and applesauce and combine.

Sauté onion, carrot, garlic, and oregano in a cast-iron fry pan with butter until onion is translucent. Sprinkle lightly with salt and generously with pepper while sautéing.

Combine onion mixture and crushed crackers with venison mixture and mix everything thoroughly.

Pack mixture firmly into a well-buttered 8½ x 4½ x 2½-inch baking dish.

Bake at 350° for 1 hour.

VENISON PATTIES

Ingredients

1½ lbs. ground venison

1 lb. ground breakfast sausage

1 medium onion, finely chopped

Bacon strips (1 per patty)

½ tsp. soy sauce (per patty)

Directions

Mix venison, sausage, and onion. Form into patties about 4 inches across and 1 inch thick. Wrap bacon around edge of each patty and pin with a toothpick where it overlaps.

Sear both sides of meat in hot skillet, and then reduce to low heat. Turn occasionally, and after turning several times, put soy sauce on each patty. Cook until meat attains desired doneness or the thermometer reads 160°.

Tip: Serve with Broccoli Cauliflower Salad (see page 151).

PAT'S VENISON CROCK-POT STEW

Ingredients

2 lbs. venison, cut into bite-size pieces

Italian salad dressing (enough to cover and marinate meat)

½ lb. bacon

1 medium onion, chopped

1 (2 oz.) packet dry onion soup mix

1 (14.5 oz.) can new potatoes

2 cups baby carrots, peeled

1 cup celery (optional)

1 T. black pepper

1 tsp. salt

1 T. garlic powder

1 (7.3 oz.) jar mushroom pieces

1 (10.5 oz.) can cream of mushroom soup

Brown rice, to serve

Directions

Marinate venison in Italian salad dressing for at least 2 hours.

Line bottom of Crock-Pot with half the bacon. Place venison in Crock-Pot and cover with remaining bacon strips. Add the onion on top of the bacon. Now dump in the dry onion soup mix. Add potatoes, carrots, and celery (if using). Add pepper, salt, and garlic powder. Add the mushroom pieces and then the mushroom soup.

Cook on low for 5 to 6 hours. Do not stir or mix up.

Prepare brown rice per package instructions.

Ladle venison mixture over brown rice and serve.

VENISON BUTTERFLY CHOPS

Ingredients

1 egg

½ cup milk

4 venison loin chops

1 cup flour

½ cup peanut oil

6 strips bacon

2 T. cooking oil from bacon

Gravy

2 cups milk

¼ cup plus 1 T. all-purpose flour

2 T. oil from wok (for the bacon
and meat flavors)

Directions

Beat egg and add milk. Set aside.

Butterfly venison loin chops and dredge them in flour. Dip them in the egg/milk mixture and dredge in flour again.

In a wok or heavy skillet, heat peanut oil and fry several strips of bacon until crisp. Remove the bacon and dry thoroughly on a paper towel. (Using a wok helps because the heat is high and it browns the outside of the chops quickly, sealing in the juices.)

Place the butterflied chops in the same cooking oil the bacon just came out of and deep-fat fry until desired doneness.

While the chops are cooking, make gravy: Whisk together milk, flour, and 2 tablespoons of cooking oil from the pan over medium heat. Stir constantly until mixture is smooth and bubbly. Continue stirring until gravy has thickened.

Serve the gravy over the chops and crumble the bacon over the gravy.

Tip: Butterfly a chop by cutting it down the middle, leaving about 1 inch at the bottom. Fold the chop over on the cutting board, creating a nice thick steak.

VENISON CUTLETS

Ingredients

Venison cutlets, cut into 4-inch
squares and ½-inch thick

Marinade

½ cup soy sauce

½ cup lemon juice

¼ cup Worcestershire sauce

Cooking Ingredients

Bacon (1 slice per cutlet)

1 cup flour

Nonstick cooking spray

Directions

Put venison cutlets in a ziplock bag.

Combine marinade ingredients and pour over meat in the ziplock bag. Marinate for 2 to 3 hours.

Remove meat from marinade and wrap each cutlet edge with a slice of bacon, pinning it with a toothpick.

Roll meat in flour and brown in hot skillet coated with non-stick cooking spray. Remove from heat and put on a baking pan.

Bake covered at 350° for 1 hour.

POOR MAN'S "VEAL-ISON"

Ingredients

1 egg, beaten

¼ cup milk

1 lb. venison steaks

1 tsp. garlic powder

1 cup breadcrumbs, seasoned

3 T. butter (or 2 T. olive oil)

Here's a recipe an old-timer gave me (Steve) years ago. When you butcher a deer, cut the steaks very thin: ⅜ inches or less. Freeze them until ready to cook (always freeze before cooking). Allow the steaks to thaw in a pan of whole milk in the refrigerator. (Never thaw venison at room temperature.)

Directions

Make egg batter by combining the egg and milk. Dip steaks in the batter.

If desired, sprinkle garlic powder on breadcrumbs. Now roll the steaks in the breadcrumbs.

Fry in butter and/or olive oil.

Tip: You'll be pleasantly surprised at how similar to veal this tastes. Serve with rice or potato and vegetable.

VENISON STEAK WITH BACON

Ingredients

1 venison steak, about 1-inch thick

3 strips bacon

Directions

Take any size venison steak and wrap with 2 to 3 strips of bacon, pinning the bacon on with wooden toothpicks. The bacon tenderizes the steaks while adding delicious flavor.

Broil steaks until bacon is crispy. Let steak rest for 10 minutes before serving.

DUTCH OVEN VENISON STEW

Ingredients

3 lb. venison, cubed

2 T. cooking oil

1 (32 oz.) can beef broth

1 tsp. salt

1 cup water

4 carrots, diced (or 1 quart
   canned carrots)

2 medium onions, chopped

4 large potatoes, cubed

Other vegetables, such as peas,
   corn, green beans

Directions

In an uncovered Dutch oven hung from a tripod over a wood fire, brown venison in cooking oil. Add beef broth, salt, and water.

Cover and cook 30 minutes.

Add carrot and onion, and cook for 30 minutes.

Add potatoes and any other desired vegetables and cook for another 30 minutes.

BARBECUED DEER RIBS

Ingredients

Sauce

2½ cups water

3 cups ketchup

1 T. white vinegar (if venison may be
   a bit gamy, increase to 3 T.)

¼ cup lemon juice

½ cup Worcestershire sauce

½ cup pure maple syrup

½ to 1 cup brown sugar

2 medium onions, diced

2 T. chili powder

½ tsp. salt

Ribs

6 lbs. venison ribs with some
   loin meat attached

Black pepper, freshly ground

Salt

Directions

Preheat oven to 325°.

Sauce

In large bowl, combine all sauce ingredients. Blend well. Taste sauce and, if desired, add up to ½ cup more brown sugar.

Ribs

Sprinkle ribs with pepper and additional salt. Double layer in 5-quart roasting pan, and roast for 1 hour.

Remove ribs from oven and pour sauce over them. Put back in oven, increase heat to 350°, and bake until ribs just begin to char on top, approximately 1½ hours.

Turn ribs over, cover pan, and bake 30 minutes longer or until ribs are tender and sauce is thick.

To serve, place ribs on platter and cover with sauce.

VENISON STEAKS IN ITALIAN DRESSING

Ingredients

5 venison steaks, cut thin

Italian dressing, enough to cover meat

Directions

Place 4 or 5 thinly cut venison steaks or butterflied backstraps in a large ziplock bag. Fill bag with Italian dressing, enough to cover meat. Refrigerate for 24 hours, turning occasionally.

Remove meat from marinade and cook slowly over a fire of mesquite, walnut, or Spanish oak. Nut, fruit, or berry wood works well also.

SCRUMPTIOUS VENISON HORS D'OEUVRES

BY PRESTON MAYO, SUBMITTED BY LABREESKA HEMPHILL

Ingredients

2 lbs. venison tenderloins

Ice water (enough to cover meat)

2 tsp. salt

8 oz. cream cheese

Jalapenos, sliced

8 oz. bacon slices, halved

Directions

Soak tenderloins in ice water and salt for 1 hour. Rinse very well to remove salt.

On each piece of raw steak place 1 teaspoon cream cheese. Top with 1 slice of jalapeno and wrap with half a slice of bacon. Pin together with a wooden toothpick.

Place on grill and cook until bacon is crispy and tenderloins reach 160°.

DANGEROUS DEER DANDER

Of all the experiences I've (Steve) had as a deer hunter, hardly any compare to what happened one late-September morning several years ago. The emotions I felt were some of the highest and some of the lowest…rather, I should say some of the scariest I've experienced.

My son, Nathan, and I got on our deer stands before daylight. We were relatively close to each other, and I was excited for both of us. It was Nathan's first time in the woods with archery equipment, and I was yet to connect to a deer with my compound bow. The woods we were in held great promise for at least one of us getting off a good shot. Needless to say, I was on the edge of my climber seat as the sun peeked over the horizon.

As it turned out, that morning we both got our first kills with a bow and arrow. Nathan's was a plump doe, and I downed what I thought was a doe but found out when I recovered it that it was a good-size button buck. Without a doubt, the fact that both of us had shared such an incredible accomplishment on the same morning provided a memory we will always treasure. But that's not where the dynamics of emotion ends.

After I found my kill, I headed to the truck to wait for Nathan to join me. When I exited the woods and looked across the field toward where I'd parked, I saw Nathan sitting on the ground, leaning against the right front driver's side tire. From a distance it looked as though he was resting. As I walked closer, I saw that he wasn't resting at all. He was trying to breathe! His lips were a pale blue, his breathing was shallow, and he barely responded when I knelt in front of him and spoke. I was baffled by his condition, but my immediate assessment was that he looked like he was having an allergic reaction to something. But what?

Nathan was around fourteen at the time. When he was younger, we found out through a few overnight stays with babysitters and friends who had cats that he had an allergy to the critters' dander. The simple solution to that dilemma was to keep cats away from him. Had he found a stray and played with it while at the truck? And then it hit me! The culprit had to be deer dander.

I quickly stood up and circled the truck. There it was. He had connected with his doe and drug it the 200 yards to the truck. The combination of a relatively warm September morning and handling the deer had created a medical emergency.

I quickly turned the truck engine on, turned the air conditioner on to maximum cool, went back to Nathan and wrestled his oxygen-starved body into the cab. I got in on my side and took off for home… and to the medicine cabinet that held the Benadryl. Thankfully, the clean, cold air provided Nathan with some immediate relief, but the drive of nearly twenty miles seemed like forever for both of us. By the time we got home, Nathan was almost breathing normally. Once we got into the house and put some medicine into his system, he returned to his regular young self.

I was completely surprised that deer dander can cause the same reaction as cat dander. And Nathan is not alone in his allergy. I've discovered since then that another friend's son had experienced the same response to deer dander. My friend and I discussed our sons' unusual struggle and managed a respectful chuckle at the thought that it was our boys' ploy to feign deer dander allergy so that their respective "old man" would do all the dragging after their shots were taken.

Eventually Nathan and I figured out that the colder the weather, the less effect deer dander had. For that reason, Nathan prefers to hunt in the colder months of the year.

By the way, you probably noted I left two deer lying on the ground when I loaded Nathan into the truck and rushed home. The good news is that after Annie and I were sure he was going to be okay, she took over his care and suggested I hurry back to the farm to retrieve our trophies. Thankfully, the meat was still good. Nathan and I enjoyed a bit of satisfaction when we consumed Annie's Famous Venison Chili that contained meat from the doe that had caused both of us such a scare.

ANNIE'S FAMOUS VENISON CHILI

Ingredients

2 lbs. ground venison

1 large onion, chopped

2 packets McCormick's Mild Chili Seasoning

1 (28 oz.) can tomatoes

1 (28 oz.) can pinto beans

Directions

Brown the meat and onion in a large skillet. Drain all fat. (I've even put the cooked meat in a colander and rinsed it off with hot water to get more fat off.)

Add the chili seasoning to the meat, stirring until mixed thoroughly. Add tomatoes and beans.

Simmer on low for at least 45 minutes. (The longer the better.)

Tip: Serve with Cornbread (see page 164).

LOUISIANA DEER CHILI

BY JAMES MAYO, SUBMITTED BY LABREESKA HEMPHILL

Ingredients

2 lbs. ground venison

2 T. olive oil

1 onion, chopped

Salt

2 T. flour

1 (10 oz.) can Rotel tomatoes
   (diced tomatoes and green chilies)

1 (15 oz.) can diced tomatoes

1 (15 oz.) can tomato sauce

2 cups water

5 T. chili powder

1 cup whole milk

1 (15 oz.) can black beans or chili
   beans (optional)

Directions

Brown meat in olive oil with onion and salt to taste. Drain.

Add remaining ingredients except milk and cook for 20 minutes.

Add milk and cook for 10 more minutes.

This is fast, easy, and delicious!

VENISON ROAST

Ingredients

5 lbs. venison roast

¼ tsp. black pepper

1 (2 oz.) packet dry onion
   soup mix

1 (10.5 oz.) can cream of
   mushroom soup

½ tsp. garlic powder

Directions

Place the venison roast on a large sheet of heavy-duty aluminum foil. Cover meat with remaining ingredients and wrap foil securely around everything to seal in heat and juices.

Bake at 350° for 4½ hours. Let set for 20 minutes before slicing so the juices will settle.

VENISON LASAGNA

Ingredients

8 oz. lasagna noodles

2 lbs. ground venison

1 medium onion, chopped

1 (32 oz.) jar spaghetti sauce

2 cups sour cream

2 cups cottage cheese

½ lb. cheddar cheese, shredded
   (or another type of cheese)

Parmesan cheese

Directions

Preheat oven to 350°.

Cook noodles according to package directions and set aside.

In a skillet, brown the venison and onion. Drain off fat. Add spaghetti sauce to the meat mixture and heat thoroughly.

In a large bowl, mix the sour cream and cottage cheese together.

Layer the ingredients in a casserole dish: noodles, meat sauce, sour cream mixture. Repeat the layers, ending with meat on top. Cover the top layer of meat with shredded cheese and sprinkle on Parmesan cheese.

Bake for 45 minutes or until the meat is bubbling and the cheese is nice and brown.

NINE MILE VENISON SLOPPY JOES

Ingredients

2 lbs. ground venison

1 (22 oz.) jar salsa

2 (10 oz.) cans tomato soup, undiluted

2 T. brown sugar (or molasses)

1 green pepper, chopped

Hamburger buns

Directions

In a large, heavy skillet, brown the ground venison until it is no longer pink. Drain the fat. Stir in the remaining ingredients and simmer for 20 minutes or until heated thoroughly.

Serve on hamburger buns.

Tip: Serve Coleslaw (page 148) on top of the sloppy joes—a West Virginia custom.

ROASTED VENISON TENDERLOIN

Ingredients

2 lbs. potatoes, quartered

1 lb. carrots, sliced on the diagonal

1 large onion, cut into chunks

2 T. canola oil, divided

2 lbs. venison tenderloin

2 tsp. dried rosemary

Salt

Pepper

Dash of Mrs. Dash seasoning

3 T. butter, melted

Directions

Mix vegetables together in a large bowl. Add 1 tablespoon canola oil and stir. Make sure all the vegetables are covered in oil.

In a heavy skillet, fry the tenderloin in 1 tablespoon canola oil until the meat is just brown.

Put the meat in a large roasting pan or casserole dish. Place the veggies around the meat and sprinkle them with the seasonings. Drizzle melted butter over the meat and vegetables.

Cover and roast at 450° for 45 minutes. Remove the cover and roast for another 20 minutes, allowing the potatoes to brown.

BEGINNER'S VENISON STEW

Ingredients

2 to 3 lbs. venison, cut into cubes

4 T. olive oil

1 T. kosher salt (kosher salt is purer and more coarse than table salt)

Pepper

6 cups water

2 T. beef bouillon, granular or cubes

2 T. Worcestershire sauce

1 (2 oz.) packet dry onion soup mix

2 tsp. garlic, minced

4 medium potatoes, quartered

6 carrots, sliced on the diagonal

4 stalks celery, chopped

3 T. cornstarch

Directions

Rinse venison in cold water and pat dry. In a heavy pot or Dutch oven, heat the oil on medium high. Salt and pepper the meat cubes, and then brown the meat in the hot oil. Add the water, bouillon, Worcestershire sauce, dry soup mix, and garlic.

Simmer for 1½ hours.

Add potato, carrot, and celery and continue to simmer until the vegetables are tender.

Just before serving, remove ½ cup of broth and mix it with the cornstarch, making sure there are no lumps. Stir the mixture back into the meat and vegetables, and simmer until the broth is thick. (You can add a little milk or a bit more beef broth if you need to thin the gravy.)

Elk

THE TEST IS IN THE TASTING

In the late 1990s, my son, Nathan, and I (Steve) went to Montana to hunt the mighty elk with guide and outfitter Randy Petrich. Annie was aware of the amount of family funds the adventure would cost us, and as the time drew near for Nathan and me to head west, I offered my best economic consolation to my dear wife. "Babe, can you really put a price tag on the value of making such memories with our son?" She nodded her head in agreement. (I had my turn to nod my head and keep my trap shut when she and Heidi took a trip to the historic town of Savannah, Georgia, a few weeks after Nathan and I returned from Montana.)

Thankfully, during the hunt Nathan and I were blessed with 6 x 6 bulls. We couldn't wait to get home and tell our tales. What made the homecoming even more special was that due to the relaxed luggage restrictions in air travel at the time, we brought both sets of antlers with us as checked baggage. We were the envy of every hunter who happened to be in the claim area when the baggage handlers brought them to us. The rest of the elk would be delivered in ten days or so (with an added cost of well over $200 for shipping).

Finally, the nearly 300 pounds of freezer-ready elk meat came to our door packed in dry ice. Annie thawed a package and used it that night as the main ingredient in her Easy Elk Stroganoff. Our family of four sat down to experience our very first meal of elk. Nathan and I were on pins and needles waiting for Annie to do the honors of taking the first taste. As she did, we wondered what she'd say. There's no way to describe the beauty of the words that came from her mouth after she slid her napkin across her lips. Perhaps a blazing red sunset behind Dexter Mountain where we took the elk might have come close to comparing with the beauty of her statement. "Boys..." She paused long enough to make us feel even more anticipation. "Boys, you're gonna have to go back and get another one. This elk is great!"

Annie smiled as Nathan and I high-fived each other. Heidi concurred with her mama's assessment of the tasty elk, and we high-fived again. Nathan and I had no trouble at all making plans to fulfill Annie's request.

ANNIE'S EASY ELK STROGANOFF

Ingredients

1 (12 oz.) pkg. egg noodles

1 lb. ground elk

1 large onion, chopped

1 (10.5 oz.) can cream of
  mushroom soup

8 oz. milk (or water)

2 T. Worcestershire sauce

8 oz. sour cream

Directions

Prepare egg noodles according to package instructions.

Crumble meat into a skillet and add the onion. Brown and drain, removing as much grease as possible. Then add the cream of mushroom soup and milk to the meat in the skillet. Pour in the Worcestershire sauce.

After heating thoroughly, add sour cream. Continue to simmer a bit longer to let flavors mingle, being careful not to allow mixture to boil.

Serve over the cooked noodles.

Tip: Family and friends who shy away from eating wild game will like this dish!

ELK ROAST

Ingredients

3 to 5 lbs. elk meat (or deer, antelope,
  caribou)

1 (10.5 oz) can cream of mushroom soup

1 (2.2 oz.) packet dry onion soup mix
  (Lipton Beefy Onion or similar flavor)

Water

Directions

Place meat in medium roaster. Add mushroom soup and soup mix with enough water to almost cover the meat.

Cover with roaster lid and bake at 325° for 3 to 4 hours, until meat is done and tender.

Serve immediately, or it's even better the next day as leftovers. To set aside for the next day, let the mixture cool, slice the meat, and place in a large casserole dish. Cover with the gravy and refrigerate overnight. Reheat to serve.

Tip: Serve with Broccoli and Cauliflower Coleslaw (page 149).

POOR MAN'S ELK STEAK

Ingredients

1 cup finely crushed cracker crumbs

1 cup milk, cold

3 lbs. ground elk

Salt and pepper

1 cup flour

3 T. butter

1 (10.5 oz.) can cream of
  mushroom soup

Directions

Mix crackers and milk thoroughly. Add elk burger and season with salt and pepper.

Form the mixture into a large patty about 1-inch thick and place on flat dish. Refrigerate overnight.

The next day, cut into serving portions and roll in flour.

In a hot skillet, brown both sides of meat mixture patties in butter. Put in a baking dish and pour mushroom soup over all.

Bake at 350° for 1 hour.

THE LONGEST NIGHT

I've (Steve) had my share of restless nights waiting to hear the results of something important to me. The nail-biting vigils have been for everything from a test score in high school to a diagnosis following a medical test, from finding out if my wife and I were approved for a home loan to discovering my name was drawn for a special hunting season. All these overnighters were tension-filled, but there is one that remains near the top of the list of most anxious waits. In this case, it involved a bull elk.

I was hunting with Rising Son Outfitter owner and guide Randy Petrich. The pursuit for elk during this hunt was with archery equipment. My friend and fellow bow hunter Eddy Richey joined us for a five-day quest. It was a Wednesday afternoon, around a quarter to six, when the action unexpectedly got hot.

We had left Spike Camp on horseback and headed down a long flat trail in the Gallatin National Forest. The plan was to slip along and do some bugling to connect with a lovesick bull. We stopped at a wallow to study the size of the hoofprints in the mud. We were sitting in our saddles when we heard a powerful bugle come from near the top of the mountain to our right. Randy said it sounded like a very mature bull. He decided to bugle back to see if he could get a response. When he blew his call, what happened next was somewhat of a blur.

Not more than 200 yards away to our left on the flat below us, a bull answered Randy's call. Our guide's eyes widened as he said, "Grab your bows and let's head downhill! He's closer now and sounds like a nice one!"

We hardly had time to hit the ground and gather around a huge pine when we heard the bull bugle again, closer this time—maybe 100 yards away. Eddy was lying on his side to minimize his profile. I was on my knees at Randy's left side, facing down the flat. Randy was also on his knees ready to repeat the cow call if needed.

Suddenly Randy spoke with an excited whisper: "He's coming in!" He looked at his two hunters to determine who could get the best shot. I was hoping Eddy would get the first shot, but Randy quickly noted that in his reclined position Eddy wouldn't have time to prepare to shoot. "Steve, knock an arrow. That bull's comin' in—and it's yours!"

In the pressure of the moment, my hands shook but I managed to click an arrow onto the string and attach the release. Then I saw the bull coming straight toward us. I thought he might walk right over us, but he turned broadside and stepped slowly behind some large trees. I judged the distance to be thirty-five yards or so.

I saw that the elk was looking down the trail in front of him and decided it was time to go to full draw. The problem was that I didn't have time to turn a little sideways to get some torque on the string like I usually do. Consequently, I had the bow straight out in front of me. I tugged with all my might, but I wasn't gaining any distance on pulling the string back. Plus, I was so rattled by the sudden encounter that all the techniques I'd practiced prior to the hunt got lost in my head. I could not put my

training into action. It seemed like the string had turned to piano wire, and all my muscles had turned to wet noodles. I was in a real dilemma. A huge elk was in range, and I couldn't get to full draw!

As if another Steve arrived on the scene to talk me back into reality, I heard, "Don't be defeated, Steve! You can get the string in position. Just pull with everything in you. *Do it now!*" So I did! And as I did, the bow shook like Jell-O on a jackhammer. About two-thirds into my draw, I was shaking so badly the arrow jumped out of its rest and fell alongside the lower riser, but still connected by its knock to the string. I was embarrassed, to say the least, as I relaxed the limbs to recover the arrow.

Randy worriedly watched as I slowly lifted the arrow back up and placed it on the pronged rest. In those few short moments of rest for my arms, I must have regained a bit of strength because when I pulled the string back again, I was surprised that I could feel the limbs yielding to my draw. Suddenly the compound bow system reached the break-over point. Instantly the pull weight dropped from sixty-five pounds to about twenty-five pounds. I was at full draw!

Amazingly, the bull was still there and had even halted. Randy said later that when the bow broke over I grunted rather loudly, and that's what stopped the bull in its tracks. For whatever reason, I was grateful to find the bull in my peep sight. But his vitals area was visible only through the forks of a tree. If I was going to take the shot, I would have to send the arrow precisely between the two trunks. There was no room for error.

I surveyed the situation for a few seconds and decided I could send the arrow safely between the forks of the tree. I also knew the bull wouldn't linger long. I settled in and felt surprisingly steady as

I pressed the trigger on the release. The bow worked perfectly, and I watched the arrow sail precisely between the tree trunks and bury into the elk. What an accomplishment!

"Did you get him good?" Randy quizzed as the bull took off and headed downhill to the flat below us.

"I believe I did. The impact sounded good!"

Eddy added his assessment that gave us pause: "From where I'm lying, I could see the arrow penetrate up to the fletching. It was a good hit, but it wasn't a pass through."

Randy offered a subdued groan at the news that there probably wasn't an exit wound, which would have caused the bull to bleed freely and die quickly.

My joy turned to concern. I was glad I was on my knees—already in praying position.

We waited a few minutes and then got up to check things out. We found a small pool of blood where the elk had been. After searching the area below us with his binoculars, Randy spotted the bull. He quietly studied the wound through the lenses and determined by the bull's behavior that my shot was a fatal hit. However, he suggested we wait two hours before moving toward the downed elk to allow it time to expire.

Finally, though it was dark, we started searching with flashlights. We quickly discovered the tough old bull still had some life in him. He jumped up and stumbled through the blackness of the forest, leaving Randy to make the only decision that made good sense. We would head back to camp and return to the scene at daylight. Thus began one of the longest nights of my life.

It would be hard to number how many times I retook the shot that night as I ate supper, washed up, and prayed. With my head on my pillow, I watched over and over and over as my arrow took off and flew between the tree trunks. I heard the thud of its impact on the elk and heard Eddy repeat, "It wasn't a pass through." I was worried.

I think I drifted off to sleep around two and the alarm sounded at four. Though I'd only slept a couple of hours, I catapulted off my cot like a jet off the deck of an aircraft carrier. I couldn't wait to get back to tracking the bull. We got to the scene of the shot, and I'm happy to report that after twenty minutes or so of searching, I heard Randy call to us from down the hill just below the flat: "Here he is!" What sweet words!

The big-bodied bull turned out to be an unusually large 5 x 5 that Randy said should be measured for a possible record-book entry in its class. I never did have it tallied, because in my estimation they don't get any bigger than they do when they come with a muscle-testing shot and a long, painful overnight wait on a quiet Montana mountain.

STEVE'S SHAKY ARMS ELK ROAST

Ingredients

3 lbs. elk shoulder or rump roast

2 cups beef broth

½ cup red wine vinegar

3 cloves garlic, crushed

1 onion, chopped

¼ cup mustard

2 T. Worcestershire sauce

2 tsp. dried thyme

6 new potatoes, quartered

1 lb. carrots, sliced

1½ T. all-purpose flour

½ cup water

Directions

Rinse the thoroughly thawed elk roast in cold water, removing as much blood as possible. Pat the roast dry and place in a large ziplock bag or glass bowl.

Mix the beef broth, red wine vinegar, garlic, onion, mustard, Worcestershire sauce, and thyme for the marinade. Cover the meat with the marinade and put in the refrigerator for 24 hours.

Place the elk and marinade in a Crock-Pot. Cook on high for 4½ to 5 hours or until meat is tender and done.

Remove the elk meat from the liquid and allow meat to sit for 10 minutes before slicing.

Remove 2 cups of broth and set aside for gravy.

Using the remaining broth, boil the potatoes and carrots until tender.

In a skillet on medium heat, mix the flour and water together. Add the reserved broth and cook until the gravy is thick.

Serve and enjoy!

"SAVE SOME FOR ME" ELK STEW

Ingredients

2 lbs. elk roast, cubed

2 T. olive oil

4 cups beef broth

2 cups cubed potatoes

2 cups finely chopped carrots

2 cups finely chopped celery

1 cup finely chopped mushrooms

1½ tsp. kosher salt

1 T. dried rosemary

3 cloves garlic, minced

½ cup red wine (or ½ cup beef broth)

Directions

Sauté elk meat in olive oil in a large skillet. Place the meat in a slow cooker. Bring beef broth to a boil in a large pot (this reduces cooking time) and add to the slow cooker. Cook on high until the meat is tender, 6 to 8 hours.

When the meat is cooked, set aside. Remove the lid and add vegetables, spices, and red wine. Add additional broth if necessary to cook the veggies.

Bring to a boil and then lower heat. Continue to cook until the vegetables are done, approximately 1 hour.

Return meat to the simmering pot of veggies and serve.

This dish is even better the second day when the flavors have had more time to mingle!

MORE THAN ONE BULLET?

Nathan and I (Steve) arrived at the Petrich family ranch midafternoon on the day before our first elk hunt. We enjoyed meeting our guide's young family, and then we unloaded our gear into the nice cabin we'd be using. Before we had unpacked everything, Randy was standing at the door with his vehicle keys in hand.

"You guys can finish this up later. Right now we need to go to the shooting range to make sure your rifles are shooting right."

My sense of humor couldn't pass up a response I was sure would get a chuckle from our hunting host. "But Randy, I can't do that. I only brought one bullet."

He didn't smile like I thought he would. Instead he replied, "Are you serious?"

Even though it seemed I had totally sideswiped Randy with my attempt at levity, I couldn't help but follow to the punch line. "Well, I know we're only allowed one elk, so I figured I only needed one bullet."

"Steve, you've got to be kidding!" The mischief in his voice gave away the fact that I was the one who'd been had. Randy had probably heard every joke and quip about the woods from hunters, and I obviously wasn't the first who had tried the "I only brought one bullet" comment. It was nice of him to play along.

As it turned out, it was a very good thing I'd brought two boxes of .270 bullets. Nathan and I used half a dozen each at the shooting range until Randy felt confident our rifles were working and our shooting skills were acceptable. A few days later, I would use up another five trying to bring down my first bull.

Nathan's kill required only two rounds. He and Randy managed to crawl within seventy-five yards of a nice 6 x 6. Nathan's first elk fell where it was standing when the shot was taken.

The next day, around five in the afternoon, on the same mountain but higher up, it was my turn. We stalked to within 250 yards of another 6 x 6. I laid my rifle across a downed log and took aim. The wind was about thirty miles per hour in my face when I pulled the trigger. Randy was watching through the binoculars and saw the bullet strike the ground about ten yards below the bull. The beast didn't even flinch. The wind was so strong and

making so much noise, the elk did not seem to have heard the shot. He had no idea we were in the area.

"Steve, take another shot but this time aim about six to eight inches over the bull above the base of the neck."

I followed his guidance, set the crosshairs above the hairline of the base of the animal's neck, and pulled the trigger. The bull hunched and then ran straight up the hill.

Randy watched him through his binoculars and gave me a post-shot report. "You hit him, but I'm not sure it was high enough in the vitals. We'll wait about thirty minutes, and then we've gotta get up this mountain to see if we can finish him off before he goes into the dark timber."

Randy soon decided thirty minutes would take us too close to sunset, so about fifteen minutes later we were sneaking up the mountain, staying just inside the pines that edged the open range where the bull had been feeding. We climbed about 1000 yards without stopping, and my Tennessee flatlander lungs felt like they were on fire. We needed to hurry.

Finally we got up on a flat and were able to crawl out to take a look at the area Randy thought the bull might have escaped to. We were a mere 200 yards from the edge of the dark timber he'd mentioned earlier. He had a worried look on his face as he surveyed the hillside. Suddenly, and thankfully, he whispered, "There he is!"

Randy quickly removed his pack and asked for mine to make a shooting rest for me to use. "Hurry! Lie down and see if you can find the bull in your scope. The window of light we need to close the deal on this bull is closing fast."

With my nerves messing with my head—and thus my eyesight—it wasn't easy to peer through the eyepiece of my scope and search the mountainside for the elk. Randy watched my barrel and kept redirecting it like a gunner's mate corrects a cannon on a battleship. Then I uttered the words he wanted to hear: "Got 'im!"

I flipped the safety off on my rifle, held steady, and fired. The light was now low enough I could see the fire leave the end of the rifle barrel. The elk stooped again and then trotted closer to the large timber.

"Shoot again, Steve!" Randy commanded.

I sent round four into the elk that was now moving slowly. Round five followed. They both connected.

Feeling quite sure the elk wouldn't get far into the dark timber, Randy said, "Let's go get your bull!" Sure enough, the brute had gone only about ten yards into the deep stand of pines before he expired. How glad I was that I had only been joking about bringing just one bullet. And that gave me some spiritual insight too.

Now I know why young David picked up five stones instead of just one when he was preparing to face Goliath. He figured he needed some backup ammo, which tells me he was more than a harp player, songwriter, and warrior. He was also a good hunter. And the fact that he still had four "bullets" left in his clip after slaying Goliath tells me he was a better shot than I am. (But I wonder if he had a thirty-mile wind in his face when he slung his first round at the giant.)

ELK CROCK-POT SUPER SUPPER

Ingredients

2 lbs. elk roast, cut into 3-inch cubes

4 large potatoes, cut into chunks

4 carrots, sliced on the diagonal

3 ribs celery, chopped

Salt and pepper

1 (10.5 oz.) can cream of
    mushroom soup

1 (10.5 oz.) soup can of water

1 (2 oz.) packet dry onion soup mix

2 tsp. garlic powder

Directions

Place meat on the bottom of the Crock-Pot. Add vegetables on top. Season with salt and pepper to your preferred taste.

Mix together the remaining ingredients and pour over the meat and veggies. Cook on low heat for 6 to 8 hours.

SWEET-AND-SOUR ELK MEATBALLS

Ingredients

1 lb. ground elk meat

1 tsp. salt

½ tsp. pepper

½ cup breadcrumbs

1 egg, slightly beaten

3 T. olive oil

Sweet-and-Sour Sauce

¾ cup ketchup

⅛ cup apple cider vinegar

⅛ cup soy sauce

¼ cup brown sugar

Directions

Mix meat, salt, pepper, breadcrumbs, and egg in a medium bowl. Form into balls and brown in hot oil. Remove the meatballs from the oil and place on paper towels to drain.

Combine the ketchup, apple cider vinegar, soy sauce, and brown sugar, mixing thoroughly.

Return the meatballs to the skillet and pour the sweet-and-sour sauce over them. Simmer for 30 minutes until the meatballs are thoroughly cooked. (Add additional water if necessary.)

TENDER ELK ROAST

Ingredients

4 to 5 lbs. elk roast

1 quart water

1 cup vinegar

3 T. salt

1 T. pepper

1 T. garlic salt

1 T. onion salt

1 T. Worcestershire sauce

1 large onion, sliced

1 (10.5 oz.) can cream of
    mushroom soup

Directions

Place the roast in a large bowl.

Mix the next 7 ingredients and pour over uncooked elk roast. Cover and marinate overnight.

Pour off juice and set aside. Place meat in a covered roasting pan. Add the juice from the marinade along with enough water so the liquid is halfway up the meat. Add the onion.

Roast for 2 hours at 350°.

Remove the meat and slice into ¼-inch thick slices. Put back into the roaster. Pour mushroom soup over the top and stir into the broth.

Bake at 300° for 2½ hours.

Tip: Serve with Sweet, Sweet Potato Casserole (page 155).

ZACH'S SLOW-COOKED ELK PEPPER STEAK

SUBMITTED BY DENA PETRICH

Ingredients

2 lbs. elk round steak

2 T. cooking oil

¼ cup soy sauce

1 cup chopped onion

1 garlic clove, minced

1 tsp. sugar

½ tsp. salt

¼ tsp. pepper

¼ tsp. ground ginger

4 tomatoes, cut into eighths, or 1 (16 oz.)
    can tomatoes with liquid, cut up

2 large green peppers, cut into strips

½ cup cold water

1 T. cornstarch

Noodles or rice

Directions

Cut steak into strips. Put oil into skillet and heat. Add steak and brown, and then transfer meat to a slow cooker.

Combine the soy sauce, onion, garlic, sugar, salt, pepper, and ground ginger. Sprinkle over elk.

Cover and cook on low for 5 to 6 hours or until meat is tender.

Add tomatoes and green peppers and continue to cook on low for 1 hour.

Combine the cold water and cornstarch to make a paste. Stir into slow cooker liquid. Cook on high until liquid is thick.

Prepare noodles or rice per package instructions.

Serve steak mixture over the noodles or rice.

ZANE'S ELK ROUND STEAK 'N' GRAVY

SUBMITTED BY DENA PETRICH

Ingredients

2 lbs. elk round steak

1 cup flour

2 T. cooking oil

1 (2 oz.) packet dry onion soup mix

1 (10.5 oz.) can cream of chicken soup

2 (10.5 Oz.) soup cans of water

Directions

Preheat oven to 350°.

Cut steak into strips and dredge in flour. Heat oil in skillet and add steak. After browning steak, transfer to an oven-safe roaster.

Sprinkle dry onion soup mix on steak. Add cream of chicken soup and spread over meat. Add enough water to cover the meat.

Bake at 350° for 3 hours.

Tip: Serve with Mashed Potatoes (page 153).

ELK BURGER SOUP

Ingredients

2 lbs. ground elk meat (or any wild game meat)

3 T. cooking oil

1 cup chopped onion

1 cup diced potatoes

1 cup diced carrots

1 cup shredded cabbage

1 (15 oz.) can stewed tomatoes

½ cup cooked wild rice

1 small bay leaf

½ tsp. thyme

1 tsp. black pepper

2 tsp. salt

2 cups beef broth

2 T. cider vinegar

1 quart water

Directions

Brown the ground elk in a skillet with hot oil, and then put meat into a large stew pot (or Crock-Pot). Add the rest of the ingredients.

Bring mixture to a boil and then reduce heat. Cover and simmer for 1½ hours (using a Crock-Pot increases cooking time). Add additional water as needed to keep meat moist.

Tip: Serve with Cornbread (page 164).

SANTA FE ELK STEW

Ingredients

3 lbs. ground elk (or venison)

2 large onions, chopped

1 green pepper, chopped

1 red pepper, chopped

2 cups sliced mushrooms

¼ cup vegetable oil

1 (15.5 oz.) can kidney beans, drained

1 (15 oz.) can black beans, drained

1 (15 oz.) can pinto beans, drained

2 (11 oz.) cans corn, drained

1 (28 oz.) can stewed tomatoes

2 cups water

1 (10 oz.) can Rotel tomatoes
    (diced tomatoes and green chilies)

2 (1 oz.) packets taco seasoning

1 (1 oz.) packet ranch dressing mix

2 T. chili powder

Salt

Pepper

This is Steve's all-time favorite use of elk or venison burger. If I'm (Annie) going to be gone for several days, he usually begs me to make a pot of this stew and a tub of Coleslaw Salad to tide him over until I get back.

Directions

Sauté the ground meat, onion, bell pepper, and mushrooms in the vegetable oil until the meat is no longer pink. Drain off excess oil. Add the remaining ingredients and simmer on high in a Crock-Pot for 3 hours or until ready to eat. The longer it simmers, the better the flavor.

Tip: Serve with Coleslaw Salad (page 149).

Moose

BAKED WESTERN MOOSE MEATBALLS

Ingredients

2 lbs. moose burger
¼ tsp. garlic powder
2 T. butter
2 eggs, beaten
1 cup milk
2 cups breadcrumbs
1 tsp. salt
½ tsp. cayenne
1 tsp. black pepper

Sauce

1 T. butter
¾ cup chopped onion
1 cup ketchup
1 OXO beef stock cube
   (or beef bouillon cube)
   dissolved in 1 cup
   boiling water
½ cup molasses
¼ cup brown sugar
⅔ cup white vinegar
2 tsp. dry mustard powder
½ tsp. salt
1 T. cornstarch

Directions

Preheat oven to 350°.

Combine first 9 ingredients and roll into 1½-inch balls. Place on a cookie sheet. Bake for 20 minutes or until cooked through. Transfer meatballs from the cookie sheet to a casserole dish or small roaster.

Combine sauce ingredients in a pot and boil until thick. Pour sauce over meatballs.

Bake at 325° for 1 hour.

MOOSE WITH SOUR CREAM

Ingredients

¼ cup flour
½ tsp. salt
½ tsp. pepper
1 tsp. garlic powder
1 lb. moose round steak, cut into
   narrow strips
2 T. cooking oil
¾ cup chopped onion
1 cup beef broth
½ tsp. thyme
1 (10 or 12 oz.) can sliced mushrooms
¾ cup peas, frozen
½ cup sour cream
12 oz. rice

Directions

Combine flour, salt, pepper, and garlic powder.

Dredge meat strips in flour mixture.

Heat oil in a deep frying pan. Brown the meat. Add onion, broth, thyme, and the liquid only from the mushrooms. Cover and simmer for 45 minutes or until meat is tender.

Add mushroom, peas, and sour cream, mixing thoroughly.

Cook over medium heat for 5 to 7 minutes.

Prepare rice according to package instructions.

Serve moose on a bed of steamed rice.

MOOSE STROGANOFF

Ingredients

1 lb. moose round steaks

1 cup flour

Salt

Pepper

¼ cup olive oil

1 cup diced onion

1 cup thinly sliced celery

1 (10.5 oz.) can cream of mushroom soup (or cream of chicken soup)

10.5 oz. milk

1 (15 oz.) can beef consommé

8 oz. mushrooms, sliced

3 T. butter

½ cup red wine (or beef broth)

1 (8 oz.) pkg. noodles

Parmesan cheese as desired

Garlic powder as desired

Directions

Beat steaks with a meat mallet to tenderize and flatten.

Mix flour, salt, and pepper. Dredge the meat in this mixture and then cut into bite-size pieces.

Heat olive oil in a skillet, add steaks, and brown. Remove steaks from skillet and place in a bowl. (Do not drain the oil from the skillet.)

Put onion and celery in the skillet and cook until almost dry, stirring frequently. Place browned meat back into the skillet to warm.

Pour cream of mushroom soup into frying pan and add milk. Add beef consommé and stir.

Simmer for 5 to 7 minutes, making sure mixture comes to a boil.

In a separate pan, sauté mushrooms in butter and red wine.

Prepare noodles according to package instructions and drain.

Serve by placing noodles on plates, adding a little butter or margarine, and then covering with the hot moose mixture. Top with mushrooms and dust with Parmesan cheese and garlic.

RHODA'S MOOSE POT ROAST

BY ALASKA RESIDENT, RHODA GRACE

Ingredients

1 T. vegetable oil

3 lbs. roast

1 cup decaf coffee (I keep a jar of instant granules in my pantry, mixes up fast)

¼ cup soy sauce

2 to 3 whole bay leaves

1 to 2 garlic cloves, finely minced

½ tsp. oregano

2 onions, divided and sliced

Additional coffee and soy sauce, as needed to replenish what evaporates.

Potatoes, 1-inch pieces

Carrots, cut to 1-inch pieces

Rice

Gravy

½ cup butter

½ cup all-purpose flour

1 cup milk

Enough beef broth and drippings from roasting pan to make a nice gravy consistency

Salt and pepper, to taste

Onion powder, to taste

This recipe is delicious with beef or venison as well. Plan to have this roast in the oven by nine in the morning, and cook on low all day so it can be served tender for dinner around four or five.

Directions

Preheat oven to 270° degrees.

Heat skillet, add a little vegetable oil, and sear meat on all sides.

In roasting pan, combine coffee, soy sauce, bay leaves, garlic, oregano, and 1 of the sliced onions.

Place meat into the pan (do not add salt until finished cooking, otherwise it will dry out your roast).

Top roast with second sliced onion. Pour some of the broth in the pan over the top of the roast.

Cover tightly with tinfoil.

Roast in oven for 8 hours, basting every hour with the juices.

Add more coffee/soy sauce with a 1:1 ratio as needed to replace juices during roasting if liquid boils away. You want quite a bit of broth in the pan to avoid burning and to use to make a gravy once the roast is finished.

Add potatoes and carrots to the broth 2 to 3 hours prior to roast being done. Add as much as will fit in your pan. Wash the vegetables first, peel if desired.

Once roast is finished, set on the counter to rest a few moments while you make rice.

Make a pot of rice. (Make as much as your crowd will need.)

While rice is cooking, make the gravy by melting the butter in a pan. When melted, whisk in flour until it has absorbed all the butter and become more of a paste. Whisk in 1 cup milk and enough beef broth from the roasting pan until a gravy consistency is reached. Season to taste with salt, pepper, and onion powder.

Shred the roast.

Place rice on a plate, top with shredded meat and roasted vegetables. Pour gravy over the top and serve with homemade bread.

Caribou

KENNETH'S CARIBOU

I've (Steve) received a lot of pictures in my mailbox and inbox from hunters who want to share their experiences. I totally enjoy each one. I like to imagine what is being said when the photos are taken because of two things I'm sure are true: 1) the animal that was taken in the picture is probably still warm, and 2) the hunter and his photographer are still basking in the glow of their success. While all the photos bring a smile to my face, there's one picture I received of a man and his downed animal that gave me as much joy as all the others combined. It featured the face of the one who introduced me to hunting way back around 1963. His name is Kenneth Bledsoe.

In my book *A Look at Life from a Deer Stand,* I shared about Kenneth inviting me to go on a squirrel hunt on an October day in West Virginia. On that morning, my future as an outdoorsman was set in place. I'll be forever grateful for his willingness to take a young, city-slicker kid into the woods to help me discover that I was born to be a hunter. Even more important, I have Kenneth to thank for

guiding me to an interest that has led to many opportunities to share spiritual "trophies of truth" I've found while engaged in hunting.

Squirrels, rabbits, deer, and grouse were plentiful on the hillsides around Kenneth's house, so he was quite content to hunt close to home. Every once in a while, he would venture to a different county in West Virginia to hunt with family or friends, but mostly his exploits were confined to Mason County. However, in his heart there was a quiet longing that was finally met. The story is best told in his own words:

> I always dreamed of going to a place to hunt and fish where I couldn't hear any planes, trains, chainsaws, cars, and tractor trailers. A place where I couldn't see anybody other than the hunter I was with. Then one day the Lord blessed me and made my dream come true. I got to go hunt the mighty Canadian caribou!
>
> I drove with my friend Maurice Pendleton from my house in West Virginia to Raddison, Quebec, on the edge of the Hudson Bay. We couldn't go any further by car, so we boarded a bush plane and flew 300 miles into the wilderness. We were 1,585 miles from my front porch! With only the sound of birds and the sight of lakes and beautiful rock formations everywhere, we camped, hunted, and fished for almost a week. It could not have been a better trip. And best of all, we both filled our caribou tags and took home some of the best meat we'll ever enjoy. May God be praised for His marvelous gifts!

As far as I'm concerned, no one deserved the trip more than Kenneth. God has some great people on the planet, and Ken's one of them in my record book! An even more enjoyable part of this story is how Kenneth's wife never wasted an ounce of her hubby's hard-earned and hard-hunted critters. Whether it was fresh rabbit, squirrel, or the season's first deer, Evelyn's skill at the skillet was amazing... and still is. Her culinary treatment of the caribou Kenneth brought home honored the effort he'd made to get it. Thankfully, she was willing to share her recipe!

EVELYN'S STEW OF CARIBOU

Ingredients

1 lb. lean caribou, chopped into
   2-inch cubes

1 quart beef stock

2 medium potatoes, peeled and diced

4 large carrots, peeled and cut into
   large chunks

3 ribs celery, cut into large chunks

2 large onions, quartered

3 large tomatoes, quartered

3 garlic cloves, finely minced

1 bay leaf

1½ cups red wine (or beef stock)

½ cup all-purpose flour

1 stick butter, melted

2 T. finely chopped thyme leaves

1 tsp. finely chopped fresh
   rosemary leaves

Salt

Pepper

Directions

Place caribou meat in a large, heavy pot. Cover with beef stock and cook on low for 45 minutes.

Add potato, carrot, celery, onion, tomato, garlic, bay leaf, and wine. (Add additional beef stock if needed to keep meat covered.) Cook until vegetables are tender, approximately 20 minutes.

In a separate bowl, mix the flour and melted butter. Add to stew (for thickening). Add rosemary, thyme, and a dash of salt and pepper. Continue to simmer for 25 minutes, allowing the flavors to mix.

KENNETH'S CARIBOU CHOPS

Ingredients

Marinade

¼ cup olive oil

1 T. Worcestershire sauce

1 T. garlic, minced

Caribou Chops

1 lb. caribou steaks, cut ½-inch thick

⅛ cup vegetable oil

1 medium onion, sliced

1 cup sliced mushrooms

1 tsp. steak seasoning

1 tsp. black pepper

Directions

Combine marinade ingredients and pour into bowl. Add steak and marinate for 24 hours.

Remove meat and pat dry.

Heat the oil in a heavy skillet on medium-high heat. Cook the steaks for 3 minutes on each side. Add onion and mushrooms, placing the steaks on top of the onion so the meat is away from direct heat. Sprinkle the steak with the seasonings. Cook until the steak and vegetables are done to your liking.

Antelope
WHERE THE ANTELOPE PLAY

Of all the animals I've (Steve) pursued in my long and enjoyable life as a hunter, the antelope is one I've yet to take. However, I've been there when one went down. Nathan, my son, and I went to Wyoming to hunt mule deer with a gentleman we met at one of our concerts. The ranch was a mere 20,000 acres, hardly enough room to turn our truck around, but we managed to have a great time. We scored on a couple of nice 4 x 4s with bodies the size of our Tennessee cows.

We were grateful for the experience and filled our deer tags early in our hunt. Since we had a couple days left to enjoy the territory, we were delighted when we learned that our host, Mr. Z, had some hunting of his own to do because he'd secured four antelope doe tags. We were privileged to go along with him.

While driving around the ranch, we topped a tall hill and came to a sudden stop. Mr. Z grunted the word "antelope," threw his door open, told us to sit still, and hurriedly grabbed his .308 Weatherby from behind the seat. He slowly walked around the back of the vehicle and appeared again at the passenger side. He walked by us and then stepped carefully to the hood of the truck and laid his rifle across it.

We looked hard for the antelope he'd seen and nearly didn't find them. To us they were little white specks in the distance. Mr. Z had a different view through his powerful scope. I watched him hone in on a target and draw a deep breath.

Nathan coughed a little bit but very quietly.

Mr. Z lifted his eye from the scope. "Boys, keep 'er quiet in there, if you will."

Nathan and I were afraid to turn our heads to look at each other, but we did. We couldn't believe that one little subdued cough might affect the crosshairs that were placed on the target we figured had to be at least 500 yards away. We'd heard of people taking 500-yard shots, but we'd never seen anyone attempt a shot that long. We held our breath while we waited for the blast of the rifle.

Finally the trigger was pulled. I thought I saw one white speck suddenly disappear, but I struggled to believe it.

Mr. Z jacked another shell into the chamber and laid his gun across the hood again. This time it was to make sure the antelope was still down. After studying the scene for a minute, he unloaded the Weatherby, recased it, put it in the back, hopped behind the wheel, and we drove to the downed antelope.

The chance to get our first mulies was exciting enough, but we never expected to get to witness a man who was so connected to his weapon. It was inspiring! Every time I go to a range now to fire my guns, I think of Mr. Z.

ANTELOPE SUPREME

Ingredients

2 lbs. antelope steak, cut into
  ½-inch cubes

3 T. olive oil

1 large onion, diced

1 cup sliced mushrooms

1 medium green pepper, diced

1 tsp. black pepper

1 tsp. kosher salt

1 tsp. garlic powder

1 (28 oz.) can stewed tomatoes

1 cup beef broth

1 T. paprika

1 T. marjoram

3 cups egg noodles, cooked

Directions

In a skillet with olive oil, brown the antelope meat. Add the onion, mushrooms, and green pepper. Stir-fry for 5 minutes or so.

In a large, heavy pot, combine the meat mixture with the remaining ingredients.

Cover and simmer for 45 minutes. Approximately 20 minutes into the simmering, prepare the noodles according to package directions and drain.

Add the noodles to the meat mixture and continue to simmer for 10 to 15 minutes. Add additional broth or water if desired.

ANTELOPE AND NOODLE SKILLET MEAL

Ingredients

2 lbs. ground antelope

1 medium onion, chopped

2 T. cooking oil

1 quart tomato juice

1 tsp. sugar

2 cups water

16 oz. noodles

1 lb. Velveeta cheese, cubed

Salt

Pepper

Directions

In a large skillet, brown the antelope and onion in oil. Drain off as much grease as possible. Add the tomato juice, sugar, and water and bring to a boil.

Add the noodles and cook until they are tender.

Turn off the heat and add the Velveeta. Cover and let sit until the cheese is fully melted. Add salt and pepper to taste.

Tip: Serve with Green and White Salad (page 149).

Bear

READY, AIM, LOAD

My (Steve) maiden voyage into the wild in search of bear could not have taken place in a more beautiful part of the planet—Montana. Eddy Richey and I joined guide Randy Petrich for a springtime trip into the mountains near Livingston. The adventure yielded one of the most unforgettable moments I've ever had…and one of the most embarrassing.

Eddy scored early in the week with a nice cinnamon-colored black bear. Though his success was ultra exciting, our rapid ascent up a mountainside to get into position for the shot nearly caused our Eastern, out-of-shape lungs to explode. With the dreaded anticipation of having to make another challenging climb for *my* chance at a shot—the news that we'd be riding horses instead was a huge relief.

With one bear already on the hook, we took off before daylight the next day. We rode a couple of hours into the high country. Around midmorning, we quietly (well, as quietly as three people mounted on horses can be) slipped through some tall pines on the way up to a point where we could set up and glass distant meadows for browsing bears. Just before we exited the thick stand of pines to cross a sizable meadow, I looked ahead and saw something unusual in the middle of the field.

"Randy!" I whispered. "Randy, stop! What is that spot in the field? Is that a panther?"

Randy pulled his binoculars up to his eyes. "Nope," he replied. "No such thing in these parts. We have mountain lions or cougars, but that darkness is the top of a black bear. He's down in a ditch. Let's dismount and stay back here in the shadows of these pines. We'll wait for him to show more of himself."

Randy had hardly finished his instructions when the bear walked out of the ditch and looked right at us. In that same instant, one of the horses decided it was time to relieve himself on the hard ground of the trail. It sounded like water from a garden hose hitting concrete. I stared at the horse and almost groaned. Randy quickly settled my fear that the bear might get nervous and take off. "It's okay, Steve. Bears can't see all that well. He probably hears the splashing, but with us being back in these shadows, I don't think he's figured out what we are. Plus the wind is blowing toward us, which is in our favor."

Then came the announcement I'd been waiting for. Without having to take another look at the bear with his binoculars, Randy said, "Steve, that bear's a big boar! He's by himself, and he's a shooter! If you want him, you'd better hurry up and get ready. He's not going to stand there very long."

Randy didn't have to say anything more. As fast as I could move, I slipped my .270 out of the saddle-mounted scabbard. I slowly approached a big, trunked pine that was about two yards in front of us. I leaned up against it for shot stability. The bear was just standing there broadside, about 75 yards out, his face turned toward me. I placed the crosshairs on his vitals. I slid the safety off, slowly pressed the trigger, and waited for the explosion to surprise me. But what I heard when the trigger mechanism dropped was bewildering and embarrassing *CLICK*. If someone had been doing live commentary on the shot, it would have gone like this: "He's ready! He's aiming! Oh oh. Now he's loading!"

In the quiet of the woods, the click sounded like a .22 rifle shot. I couldn't believe it. In the excitement of the moment, I'd forgotten the most important component of the deal closer—having bullets in the gun. My rifle wasn't loaded because I'd been following Randy's safety policy (good for man and horse) of not chambering a bullet until the opportunity for a shot was presented.

Eddy was filming the entire debacle, and I knew Randy was watching me. I kept my eye on the bear and slowly felt for the bolt of the rifle. I'm not sure, but I think I heard some snickering coming from the peanut gallery. (Perhaps it was coming from the horses…) The bear continued to stare in our direction, still standing broadside, as if waiting for me to get my act together.

It's hard to subdue the sound of metal sliding against metal, but I managed to get a round into the chamber without spooking the beast. With the gun now loaded, I checked the safety once more. I lowered my eye to the scope rim and aimed. When I pulled the trigger this time, I felt the jolt of the shot against my shoulder. I watched through the scope as the bear fell right where it had been standing. The deal was done. All that was left to do was put up with the anticipated one thousand comments about my goof from the two onlookers. And even more distressing was that I knew the moment was captured on film.

Randy later commented on how composed I seemed in the face of the blunder. He was being a nice man. So how do I feel about my "ready, aim, load" moment today? While it wasn't one of my more stellar performances as a hunter, I'm grateful for the outcome. (I'm sure the bear regretted it though.) As I often do, I looked for a good lesson to take away from the experience. I did find one that I kept repeating to Randy and Eddy each time they poked me with their fun stick. You're welcome to use it too when you need it: "Greatness is not found in perfection; it's found in recovery."

COUNTRY-STYLE BEAR STEAKS

Ingredients

Bear steaks

Marinade (see Gravies, Marinades, and Sauces, page 185)

1 tsp. salt

½ tsp. pepper

1 tsp. garlic powder
  (or 3 garlic cloves, crushed)

1½ cups flour

½ cup cooking oil

1 (2 oz.) packet dry onion soup mix
  (or ½ cup chopped onion)

Water

Warning: Approximately 5 percent of black bears carry trichinella spiralis, a parasite known to cause trichinosis. To avoid this health hazard, be sure the meat is cooked and handled properly. The safest way to eat bear meat is to make sure it is cooked until it falls off the bone, until it is fork tender.

Directions

Marinate the bear steaks in your favorite marinade.

Remove the meat and rinse with cold water. Pat dry.

Slice the steaks into desired portions, approximately ¼-inch thick. Using a tenderizing meat mallet, pound the meat until tender.

Add the salt, pepper, and garlic powder to 1 cup of flour. Dredge the steaks in the flour mixture.

Heat the oil on medium-high in a skillet with a lid. Brown the bear meat for 2 to 3 minutes on each side. Add the dry onion soup mix and enough water to cover meat. Cover tightly and simmer until meat is tender, approximately 1 hour.

Uncover and gradually add additional flour until the liquid in the skillet thickens to a nice gravy consistency.

Tip: The tenderness of bear meat depends on the age of the bear. When preparing meat from a young bear, marinating isn't necessary, although it will tenderize and help remove any gamy taste. Meat from older bears should always be marinated before cooking. Bear meat is great in casseroles and stews too.

BEAR STEW

Ingredients

Meat Preparation

Bear meat, cut into 1-inch squares

1 cup flour

½ cup cooking oil

Stew Preparation

Vegetables of choice: onion, carrot, potato, tomato, etc.

1 quart beef broth

2 to 4 T. flour

2 T. dried parsley

1 tsp. dried sage

Warning: To avoid parasites, it is imperative that bear meat is cooked and handled properly. The safest way to eat bear meat is to make sure it is cooked until it falls off the bone, until it is fork tender.

Directions

Meat Preparation

Like all wild game, the gamy taste of bear meat is from the fat and connecting tissue. Here's a great way to prepare bear:

Cut the meat into 1-inch squares, roll in flour, and fry in hot oil until brown on the outside.

Place the bear meat in a large pot and cook (boil, bake, or Crock-Pot) until it is tender and falling apart.

Put the bear meat in the refrigerator and let cool until the next day.

Take the meat out and scrape away the fat.

Stew Preparation

Dice vegetables you plan to use. In a large pot, boil the vegetables in the beef broth on medium heat for 15 to 20 minutes. If you're including tomato, add them during the last 5 minutes of the cooking time.

Add the bear meat and let the meat and vegetables simmer together for 45 minutes.

Add flour to thicken the broth to make gravy. Start with 2 tablespoons of flour and add more until desired consistency is attained.

Add the parsley and sage. Simmer 5 more minutes and serve.

BLACK BEAR BOLOGNA

Ingredients

4 lbs. ground bear meat

¼ cup Morton's Tender Quick Meat Cure

3 tsp. sugar

1 T. lemon pepper

½ T. black pepper, freshly ground

Warning: To avoid parasites, it is imperative that bear meat is cooked and handled properly. The safest way to eat bear meat is to make sure it is cooked until it falls off the bone, until it is fork tender.

Directions

Mix all ingredients well and refrigerate overnight in a ziplock bag.

The next day form the meat mixture into 1-pound rolls.

Using a cold smoker, smoke meat for 3 hours. Finish by cooking the meat on a gas grill for 45 minutes or so. Be careful not to overcook, but make sure the meat is done inside.

Cool, slice, and eat.

Tip: Although bear meat is best for this recipe, caribou, deer, and snow goose also work.

PREPARING BEAR BREAKFAST SAUSAGE

Ingredients

1 lb. bear breakfast sausage

3 T. cooking oil

½ cup diced green pepper

4 flour tortillas

Directions

In a skillet with oil, brown the bear breakfast sausage. Add green pepper and mix.

Spoon mixture into a tortilla and roll up like a burrito.

Tip: The bear is a member of the pork family, so be sure the meat is thoroughly cooked—at least to 170° throughout to kill any parasites. Or make sure the meat is stored at -10° for at least 30 days.

JOE'S BIG BEAR

AS TOLD BY JOE EMMERT

I shot my 350-pound black bear in September of 2006 near Red Lake, Ontario, Canada. It was on the first day of a one-week hunting and fishing trip. To get there, we drove about five hours north of International Falls, Minnesota. That's where all roads north in that area end. On the first afternoon of our hunt, I'd only been in my treestand around five minutes. I barely got settled down when I saw motion through the trees. It was black and materialized into a bear—a big one!

The bear slowly came into range. I fired one round from my rifle. The big black bulldozer took off! I lowered my gun and quickly climbed down from the stand. I reloaded and followed the freshly made path of the bear through the thick underbrush. Believe me, since I didn't see the bear fall, my heart was pounding its way up my throat as I looked for him. And, yes, my finger was poised on the safety, ready to click it off and shoot if I had to. Finally, I saw it. As I approached the mountain of black fur, my imagination threatened to make me believe the bear was still breathing. But it wasn't.

I tried to call my hunting partners on my walkie-talkie but was out of range. To get a little more height for the antenna, I went back to my treestand. I reached base camp and asked for help.

When the help finally arrived, we headed to my bear. It was all the four of us could do to get that big fella into the boat to go back to camp!

Since I'd taken the bear on the first day of the trip, I had nothing to do but watch the eagles, fish for walleye, and enjoy the sunsets over Red Lake for the rest of the week. It was a hard job, but someone had to do it.

Thanks to plenty of good coolers and lots of dry ice, we made a legal immigrant of that bear. My family enjoyed the meat for quite a while. I continue to enjoy the bear rug on the wall, but the best part of the experience is telling the story to my grandchildren—with some grandfatherly exaggerations for the sake of drama thrown in, of course.

JOE'S BIG BEAR ROAST

Ingredients

2 to 4 lbs. bear roast

2 cups water with 1 tsp. salt

1 quart tomato juice

¾ cup brown sugar

2 T. Worcestershire sauce

½ tsp. black pepper

½ tsp. celery seed

1 medium onion, diced
   (Georgia Vidalia is best)

Warning: To avoid parasites, it is imperative that bear meat is cooked and handled properly. The safest way to eat bear meat is to make sure it is cooked until it falls off the bone, until it is fork tender.

Directions

Boil the bear roast in the saltwater, and then let the meat simmer for 30 minutes. Drain the fat and water. Wash away any fat or grease residue.

Place the bear meat in a Crock-Pot. Cook on high heat for 2 hours or low heat for 4 hours. Drain off visible fat.

Add the rest of the ingredients to the Crock-Pot and simmer for at least 4 hours.

Tip: Make Poor Man's Gravy (page 186) using some of the liquid in the Crock-Pot. Serve with Mashed Potatoes (page 153) and Broccoli Cauliflower Salad (page 151).

BEAR BREAKFAST SAUSAGE

Ingredients

Bear meat

1 pork chop (per 2 pounds of bear meat)

Per quart of meat:

2 T. poultry seasoning

1 tsp. salt

1 tsp. pepper

1 T. Cajun spices (optional, instead
   of salt and pepper)

Warning: To avoid parasites, it is imperative that bear meat is cooked and handled properly. The safest way to eat bear meat is to make sure it is cooked until it falls off the bone, until it is fork tender.

Directions

Grind the bear meat without seasoning. Add a deboned pork chop for each 2 pounds of bear meat.

Grind the meat again, this time mixing in poultry seasoning, salt, and pepper. If preferred, Cajun spices can be used instead of salt and pepper.

Divide the prepared sausage into 1-pound packages that can be frozen until used.

Bison (Buffalo)

I'll (Steve) never forget the look on Annie's face when she took her first bite of buffalo burger. We were at a wild game dinner where I was the keynote speaker. My "deer" wife became an instant fan of the mighty buffalo. From that meal on, she's had a bison bent. However, we discovered an issue we didn't expect. When it comes to bison, the cost per pound can rival the full weight of the animal! Knowing this makes us extra grateful for our generous buffalo-hunting friends who love to share.

SIMPLE AND TASTY BISON BURGERS

Ingredients

1 lb. ground bison

1½ tsp. kosher salt

½ tsp. black pepper

3 T. cooking oil (do not use olive oil)

1 pkg. hamburger buns

Directions

Spread the ground bison on a cookie sheet, and sprinkle salt and pepper evenly. Shape the burger into patties. Avoid over-handling the meat, which can make it less tender.

Place the patties on a large plate, cover with plastic wrap, and allow to rest in the refrigerator for at least 1 hour.

Cook on a greased grill or skillet until the internal temperature of the burger reaches 160°.

Tip: A mature buffalo bull will average 1500 to 2000 pounds. The yield of meat for cooking can easily be in the hundreds of pounds.

BISON COUNTRY-FRIED STEAKS

Ingredients

1 lb. bison steaks, cut ½-inch thick

16 oz. Coca-Cola

1 tsp. dry steak seasoning

1 tsp. coarse ground black pepper

¾ cup all-purpose flour

¼ cup canola oil

1 small onion, chopped

1 cup sliced mushrooms

1 cup milk

Directions

Pound the bison steaks with a mallet to tenderize the meat.

Marinate the bison meat for 24 hours in Coca-Cola (or another marinade, see "Gravies, Marinades, and Sauces," page 185).

Remove the bison from the marinade and pat dry.

Combine steak seasoning and pepper with ½ cup flour. Dredge the meat in the mixture.

In a large, heavy skillet, heat the canola oil on medium-high. When oil is hot, add the bison steaks, cooking on both sides until golden brown, approximately 4 minutes per side. Set aside.

Gravy

Brown the onion and mushrooms in the skillet of drippings from frying the bison. Stir in 2 tablespoons of flour and add the milk. Stir and simmer until thick.

Tip: Serve with Mashed Potatoes (page 153) and hot Sylvie Biscuits (page 163) for a great meal.

BISON AND MUSHROOM PASTA

Ingredients

4 tsp. vegetable oil

1 tsp. chili powder

4 (6 oz.) bison steaks

3 T. butter

8 oz. smoked ham, cut into strips

8 oz. mushrooms, sliced

1 (12 oz.) pkg. linguine

4 oz. heavy cream

Directions

Mix the oil and chili powder together and rub on steaks. Allow meat to rest for 30 minutes.

In a heated saucepan, sear the steaks on both sides. Lower heat and cook until desired doneness, making sure steaks are cooked all the way through. Turn the steaks often.

Melt the butter in a sauté pan. Cook the ham and mushrooms until mushrooms are limp, approximately 4 minutes.

Prepare linguine according to package instructions and add it to the ham and mushroom mixture. Heat thoroughly, stirring constantly. Stir in the cream and heat until hot.

To serve, place fried bison on top of pasta or serve pasta as a side dish.

BISON STEAKS

Ingredients

2 lbs. bison steaks

2 T. butter

8 oz. mushrooms, sliced

2 cloves garlic, minced (or ½ cup chopped onion)

½ cup cooking wine

Directions

In a frying pan, brown both sides of the steaks in butter. Cook until the meat is rare or medium rare. Remove meat from pan and set aside to rest.

Add more butter to the skillet, if necessary, and sauté mushrooms and garlic until soft and brown. Add the cooking wine and stir for 5 minutes, allowing the flavors to mingle and the liquid to be absorbed by the vegetables. (Most of the alcohol in the wine will dissipate during cooking.)

Add the steaks to the sautéed ingredients and continue to cook until meat attains desired doneness.

Tip: Top steaks with Homemade Barbecue Sauce (page 192) or Sweet Red Onion Marmalade (page 194).

Wild Boar

TIPS FOR COOKING WILD BOAR

- Wild boar meat contains much less fat than domestically raised pork. The wild boar meat will be darker and have a different consistency. If the meat is prepared properly, it will be just as tasty.

- Trim away as much fat as possible. This means you may need to add oil or butter when cooking to keep the meat from becoming too dry.

HONEY-GLAZED WILD BOAR STEAKS OR CHOPS

Ingredients

2 large boar steaks or 7 chops

Honey

Oven bag

1 packet seasoning of choice (try McCormick's Bag and Season for pork chops)

Directions

Coat wild boar steaks or chops with honey. Following the oven bag instructions, place the meat in the oven bag. Follow the seasoning package directions and then pour into oven bag.

Cook according to the directions for pork that came with the oven bag. (Usually pork steaks cook at 350° for 30 minutes or so.) Or instead of gravy, try dipping the meat in applesauce.

WILD BOAR CHOPS

Ingredients

6 wild boar chops

Marinade

1 (12 oz.) can beef broth

2 cups cider vinegar

2 cups water

1½ tsp. black pepper

2 tsp. salt

2 bay leaves

1 tsp. dried thyme

2 cloves garlic, chopped

½ cup cranberries

Main Ingredients

7 carrots, sliced on the diagonal

2 large onions, quartered

4 ribs celery, sliced

1 (12 oz.) can beef broth

⅓ cup currant jelly

½ cup all-purpose flour

Directions

In a large glass bowl, combine the marinade ingredients. Add meat to the marinade, cover, and refrigerate for 36 to 48 hours. Turn the meat every few hours.

Pour the meat and marinade into a large, heavy kettle. Cover and simmer on stove for 2½ hours or until meat is almost tender. Add the vegetables and cook until done. (If you use a Crock-Pot, cook on high for 6 to 8 hours.)

Remove the meat and vegetables from broth and cover them to keep warm.

Add beef broth, currant jelly, and flour to the marinade, still heating on the stove. Stir until the sauce bubbles and thickens to gravy consistency.

Pour gravy over the meat and vegetables and serve.

12-HOUR WILD BOAR CHOPS

Ingredients

6 wild boar chops

1 (16 oz.) can chicken broth

1 (10.5 oz.) can cream of chicken soup

4 medium potatoes, cut into chunks

4 carrots, diced

2 medium onions, diced

Salt, pepper, and garlic powder to taste

Directions

Place chops in a large pan. Pour chicken broth over chops.

In a bowl, mix the cream of chicken soup per directions on the can. Pour it over the chops as well.

Add the potatoes, carrots, and onions. Stir in the spices.

Bring mixture to a slow boil.

Pour the mixture into a Crock-Pot and let simmer on low for a full 12 hours, checking periodically to see if more water is needed to keep meat covered. (Wild boar chops and steaks tend to be tough, but using this method makes them tender and tasty.)

WILD "BOARGERS" AND HONEY-GLAZED ONIONS

Ingredients

⅓ lb. ground wild boar sausage
   (per person)

1 hamburger bun (per person)

Condiments as desired

Honey-Glazed Onions

Golf ball-size onions, any type,
   cut into quarters (2 per person)

½ cup water

1 T. vegetable oil

½ tsp. salt

2 T. honey

If you love onion, you'll love this dish. Serve boar sausage burgers on hamburger buns, along with other fixins, such as French fries, pickles, and ketchup.

Directions

Boarburgers

Form ⅓-pound patties and cook on grill to desired doneness. Serve with all the fixins for hamburgers.

Honey-Glazed Onions

Cut the stems and root ends from onions, and then peel them.

Place onions in a wok or cooking pan with water and vegetable oil. Sprinkle with salt. Cover and cook until the onions are soft, approximately 5 minutes.

Remove onions from pan and place in a small bowl. Allow to cool.

Just before serving, place the bowl of onions in the microwave and reheat until the onions are steaming hot. Remove from microwave, drizzle a small amount of honey over them, and serve.

Part Two

SMALL GAME

 Raccoon

AN UNLIKELY FOOD SOURCE

While there are lots of game we could include in this book, we've chosen one you might not have considered. We include this one for sentimental reasons. It was a flavor favored by N.R. Williamson, Annie's dad. His affection for this particular animal was likely a result of remembering how it met a very real need when he was growing up and food was scarce at times.

The smell of this critter baking in the oven seemed to evoke treasured memories of his earlier years when he spent nights chasing this critter with his brothers and their rambunctious hounds. Knowing his appreciation for this food source, his wife, Sylvia, graciously accommodated his occasional hankering by serving Baked 'Coon.

BAKED 'COON

Ingredients

1 raccoon

1 tsp. salt

½ tsp. black pepper

½ tsp. red pepper

½ cup chopped onion

½ tsp. powdered garlic

1 T. rubbed sage

1 T. Worcestershire sauce

3 sticks butter

10 medium sweet potatoes, peeled
  and baked

2 T. sugar

Directions

Boil the raccoon meat in a large pot of water until very tender, 1 to 2 hours, depending on the size of animal. Remove from water and drain.

Scrape off all fat, remove scent glands (these 4 "kernels" are the size of kidney beans, look brown and waxy, and are located under the forelegs and along the small of the back).

Cut the 'coon into sections and place in a large, shallow baking pan. Dust on all sides with salt and black and red pepper. Add onion, garlic, sage, Worcestershire sauce, and 1 stick of butter.

Set potatoes firmly on top of 'coon meat and sprinkle with sugar. Baste liberally with remaining butter.

Broil for approximately 20 minutes or until brown.

Remove from oven, turn meat over, and broil again until that side is brown.

Serve hot.

Tip: Serve with Tomato Gravy (page 186).

Squirrel

SMALL BEGINNINGS

When I (Steve) was introduced to hunting way back in the old days, there were very few deer in my part of the world. In fact, whenever someone sighted a whitetail, the phones started ringing in the valley and the news spread quickly. Because opportunities for hunting big game were so limited, we had to be content with chasing smaller critters. Thankfully, they were plentiful.

While there were sufficient numbers of squirrels, not everyone regarded them as edible. Some folks considered squirrels nothing more than large rats with bushy tails. But because they were plentiful and the meat provided a money-saving supplement of food, people were willing to learn to like eating them. But for some people, a stretching of their taste buds was required to sit down and eat a meal that included this delicacy.

Fortunately, my introduction to eating squirrel took place in the dining room of the wife of the man who took me hunting for the first time. Kenneth's wife, Evelyn, has mastered the art of cooking squirrel so well that Kenneth would even crack open squirrel skulls to eat the brains. (I tried them, but I never developed a taste for it.) My first supper at the Bledsoe table with squirrel on the menu was so lip-smackin' good that from then on I was a fan of the furry little critters.

I contacted Evelyn and asked her to share her story of how she came to be such an expert with small game.

LEARNING TO LOVE SQUIRREL AND THE MAN WHO LOVES TO HUNT THEM

BY EVELYN BLEDSOE

Because no one in my family hunted, and none of us had ever eaten wild meat, I didn't realize that people actually ate the animals that roamed the fields and woods. But then I married a fine young man named Kenneth. About a month after our wedding, hunting season began. As it approached, I learned the reality of how opening day affects a dedicated hunter and those he loves sharing the season with.

Kenneth, his dad, his grandfather, and several of his brothers constantly talked and planned where they'd hunt the first day—what time to be in the woods, what guns to use, what ammo, what the correct clothing would be, and on and on. They also talked about how they looked forward to their hunting successes being turned into tasty meals. That last item really got my attention.

As a newlywed, I'd just started learning how to cook. I could manage familiar meals, such as pork chops, mashed potatoes, and canned veggies. And I was slowly learning the art of cooking beef and chicken. But rabbits? Squirrels? Groundhogs? Even frogs? O my, what a challenge! I knew there'd be no way to change my man's taste for all things wild, so I resolved to learn the art of cooking wild game.

One of the first lessons I learned about making a great meal of small game was "gravy is the key." My husband had grown up on his mother's wild gravy, and he kindly made it clear that he wanted me to learn how to make it. He was even helpful enough to stay in the kitchen as I tried, giving me tips on how his mother had done it. After each attempt, we would mutually decide what could be done differently the next time to get the desired results. We'd add more grease, sometimes more flour, or we'd try cooking it longer. This learning process went on for months.

Finally, one evening we got a batch of gravy that generated that smile every wife loves to see on her husband. When Kenneth tasted it, he said, "That's it!" I knew his proclamation meant it was as close to his mother's recipe than any we'd made so far.

A few weeks later we again ate squirrel and gravy—this time at my in-laws' house. On the way home, my darling husband said something that was even sweeter than "That's it!" He said, "The gravy we made tasted better than Mom's!" Woo hoo! I knew I had truly arrived. It was a major culinary success.

That red-letter day happened more than 55 years ago. Yes, I'm still making wild gravy for my husband—and all our kids and grandkids. And yes, they all hunt, bringing the critters in for me to cook. Even my granddaughter hunts. I've told them all that somebody in the family needs to learn to make my special gravy before I'm gone, but they don't stop eating long enough to let me teach them. They're too busy smacking their lips and diving in for seconds!

BLEDSOES' FAVORITE SQUIRREL AND GRAVY

Ingredients

2 squirrels, cut into serving-size
    pieces (include heads if possible)
Water with 4 T. salt
Dried red pepper flakes

Gravy
2 T. solid shortening
4½ T. flour
Water

Directions

The night before, put the squirrel meat in a 3-quart pan and add enough saltwater to cover. Let sit in the refrigerator overnight.

When ready to cook the squirrel, pour out the salt water. Rinse the meat with clean water.

Return the meat to the same pan, add water to cover the meat by about 3 inches. Add salt and red pepper flakes to taste. Bring to boil, and then reduce heat and let it simmer until done, about 2 hours. Watch closely. You may need to add extra water to keep the meat covered. Also, don't cook too long or the meat may fall off the bones.

When the squirrel is done, place it in a bowl and set aside. You should have 2 or 3 cups of water left in the pan to use for the gravy.

Gravy

In a large iron skillet, melt the shortening with medium heat. Add the flour a little at a time, stirring constantly. When flour is absorbed by the grease, let it brown well. Keep stirring so it doesn't burn. Add more flour or shortening to even out the ingredients and get the right gravy consistency. (Do not use milk! Milk covers the squirrel taste you want.) Taste the gravy and add salt and pepper if needed.

Let the gravy cook slowly for 25 to 30 minutes, stirring often and adding water if needed.

While the gravy is simmering, coat the squirrel meat with flour. Put the meat in another skillet with a little shortening. Brown it on both sides.

Serve the squirrel with the gravy.

Tip: Evelyn, Steve, and Annie's challenge to you: Many years ago when funds were limited, we let nothing go to waste when we ate wild game. We consumed squirrel brains, which are considered by some a delicacy. To eat squirrel brain, crack the skull with a table knife, pull the bone away, and slurp out the brain. We double-squirrel dare ya! If you take the dare, don't be surprised if you get a sudden urge to climb trees and dig for acorns.

CROCK-POT SQUIRREL

Ingredients

4 to 6 squirrels, cut into
  serving-size pieces

¼ cup soy sauce

¼ cup of water

¼ cup brown sugar

3 T. lemon or lime juice

¼ tsp. garlic powder

¼ tsp. ground ginger

1 cup flour

Directions

Place the squirrel in a Crock-Pot.

Mix rest of ingredients (except flour) together and pour over the meat.

Cover and cook all day on low heat until tender.

Pour Crock-Pot contents into a skillet. Add flour and cook on top of the stove until the broth thickens into gravy.

Tip: Serve with Mashed Potatoes (page 153) and Sylvie Biscuits (page 163).

MR. ROGERS'S BENT BARREL

Annie and I (Steve) attended the same junior and senior high in Point Pleasant, West Virginia. Our shared past has an advantage we cherish: We enjoy remembering faces and names we both know. Among the many people we recall from time to time is the biology teacher I had in the ninth grade. His name was Mr. Jack Rogers. Although Annie didn't have the opportunity of having him as a teacher, she remembers how kind he was to all the kids outside the classroom.

Perhaps one of the reasons he was a favorite teacher was because he would often take his classes outside for a hands-on lesson in biology. Not only did our field trips make the subject more interesting, hardly anything could make a junior high kid happier than not sitting in a classroom. We knew it was going to be a great hour of school when Mr. Rogers would lead us down the hall, through a side door, and out into the sunshine. Sometimes he would herd us to a nearby patch of woods where we would look at the unique growth of ground cedar and mosses. Or he'd guide us to a small field where we would study wildflowers. On another day he might lead us to someone's front yard near the high school, with their permission, where we would huddle under an oak tree to learn about its leaf structure and the power within an acorn.

On more than one occasion, as we made our way back to the school building, he would talk with us about his other interest—sports. He so enjoyed discussing all types of sports that it was tempting for him to spend more class time talking about them than teaching biology. In fact, knowing that Mr. Rogers was always ready to discuss sports, some students would attempt to delay learning by bringing up the subject when they first walked into class. Their hope was that his play-by-play recap would replace boring stuff, such as learning the olfactory system of the common mouse. But Mr. Rogers was much more savvy than the students, and he didn't allow that tactic to work except on a few deliberate occasions.

Mr. Rogers turned his love of football, baseball, and basketball into an opportunity to garner some local and regional fame. When he wasn't teaching or grading tests, our biology guru was writing the daily sports column for our town newspaper. Because he had a gift for turning the regular stats of a game and other sports-related stories into tall tales, his articles were rarely missed by subscribers. No local sport was left uncovered in his column, and for those of us in his classroom who preferred hunting, we were always glad to get a mention.

The newspaper published one of his far-fetched yarns just after squirrel season opened in the mid-60s. Mr. Rogers tested the story on us first—a classroom filled with mostly gullible, nonhunting teenagers. I was in the room when it happened, but I'm glad to report that I, along with a couple of other young squirrel chasers, wasn't fooled by him. His story went something like this.

> Yep. Went squirrel huntin' over the weekend. It was good to get out there again, but there weren't a lot of bushytails in the woods. In fact, I only saw one. It came down a big red oak. I raised my shotgun to take him, and the scoundrel saw me and ran

around the tree. I couldn't see him, but I could hear him squawking at me. He protested my presence for probably five minutes or more. Kinda made me mad. I figured he wasn't going to show himself again, so while he was hollerin' I took my gun and put the front part of the barrel over my knee. I pulled on it with both hands and bent that sucker into the shape of the letter "J." Then I crawled up real quiet to the backside of that oak. That squirrel was makin' so much noise, he didn't hear me coming. I figured out he was about six feet off the ground with his back toenails dug into the bark, just hanging there yappin'. I stood up and slipped that bent barrel around the right side of the tree real slow and pulled the trigger. I watched that squirrel fly off to my left and land in the leaves—deader than a doornail.

When he finished the story, my hunting buddy and I surveyed our fellow classmates to see who was believing Mr. Rogers's story. We could tell some were totally amazed at his incredible ingenuity and strength! The funniest part to me was that after the story, Mr. Rogers went on to the day's lesson. He never broke into a mischievous grin or gave a hint that his tale was a complete fabrication.

To this day I wonder how many of the students in the classroom have grown up, gotten married, had kids, and shared that story with them. I know I've told it to my own—and just like Mr. Rogers, I let them believe every word.

MR. ROGERS'S SQUIRREL JAMBALAYA

Ingredients

1 squirrel

Salt

Red pepper

3 T. oil

2 large onions, chopped

3 ribs celery, chopped

1 clove garlic, minced

¼ green pepper, chopped

4 tsp. parsley, chopped

1 cup uncooked rice

1½ cups water

Directions

Cut squirrel into serving pieces, season with salt and red pepper while sautéing the meat in oil until brown. Remove from skillet.

Sauté onion, celery, garlic, green pepper, and parsley in the skillet until veggies are wilted.

Put squirrel back into the skillet, cover, and cook until tender.

Add rice and water and cook until the rice is done.

Rabbit

In West Virginia where I (Steve) grew up, rabbit hunting came well after squirrel season, which usually opened in October. For that reason, by the time we were allowed to go to the fields to beat the brush in pursuit of cottontails, the weather had turned cold. Because of the frigid temperatures, rabbit hunting was ideal because we did a lot of walking instead of sitting still and waiting like we did for squirrel and deer.

In addition to a type of hunt that doesn't require stillness, we could take dogs along to find and move the rabbits for us. What luxury to have two or three good, well-trained beagle hounds to rustle rabbits out of their hiding places. Hunting without dogs was an exercise in exercise. A day without dogs meant we would have to jump up and down on brush piles and cover every inch of grassy ground to stir up the rabbits. That kind of hunting left us sweaty and exhausted from...well...acting like dogs. So it goes without saying that a good hunting beagle was worth its weight in gold.

I hunted rabbits a lot in my teen years with my mentor, Kenneth Bledsoe. I also spent a fair amount of time chasing bunnies with his young neighbor Greg Bonecutter. We made a ton of memories, but time went on and eventually responsibilities such as college, the navy, marriage, kids, and work became my focus (and rightly so). Time spent rabbit hunting declined.

About once a year, the rabbit-hunting itch was scratched when our family would drive to West Virginia to see our parents and siblings. I got to hunt with Annie's brothers. Even those chances to chase rabbits dwindled as the years went by. But whenever the opportunity presents itself, I still enjoy chasing the furry critters. And sitting around enjoying a delicious rabbit meal with family and friends is always something to look forward to.

TIPS FOR COOKING RABBIT

- B-Be aware of the BBs. Most of us hunt rabbits with a shotgun using shells that are filled with lead or steel BBs. For that reason, it is imperative to check the meat thoroughly for the shot so that the folks who enjoy the cooked version of the critter won't have to get up from the table and make an emergency trip to a dentist. You can usually track the presence of a BB in the meat by looking closely for small, bruised slits (sometimes round) on the outside of the muscle. Some entry wounds might be filled with rabbit fur gathered by the BB on the way in. The BBs and any residual fur can be removed with a sharp, pointed knife.

- Any good chicken recipe can be used when preparing rabbit. However, because there is so little fat on the meat, you may want to use additional butter or oil when browning or basting the meat.

- Remove the scent glands. To help minimize the gamy taste of rabbit, clean out all blood and blood clots under cool running water. Remove the small scent glands (small, waxy-looking kernels under the forelegs and on both sides of the spine), being careful not to cut into them. After skinning, cut the meat into quarters. Dry the pieces and refrigerate as soon as possible. Use within three days or freeze the meat for later use.

ROSEMARY ROASTED RABBIT

Ingredients

1 rabbit, quartered

½ cup olive oil

Salt

Pepper

½ cup white cooking wine

2 whole garlic cloves

1 sprig dried rosemary

Directions

Preheat oven to 375°. Coat the rabbit pieces with oil and season with salt and pepper.

Place the rabbit pieces in a roasting pan and pour the wine over it. Add garlic and rosemary and cover with foil.

Bake for 1½ hours.

HASENPFEFFER (A GERMAN RECIPE FOR RABBIT)

Ingredients

1 large onion, sliced

3 cups white vinegar

3 cups water

1 T. pickling spices

2 tsp. salt

1 tsp. pepper

1 large rabbit, cut into
   serving-size pieces

½ cup all-purpose flour, divided

4 or 5 slices of bacon

2 T. butter or margarine

Directions

In a large glass bowl, combine onion, vinegar, water, and seasonings. Add rabbit pieces. Cover and refrigerate for 48 hours, turning occasionally.

Remove meat, strain the liquid, and set aside.

Dry the meat well and then coat lightly with ¼ cup flour. Place the rabbit and bacon strips in a heavy roasting pan.

Bake at 350° for 1 hour. Remove the rabbit and place on a warmed platter.

In a separate pan, melt the butter and gradually stir in 2 cups of the marinade. Stir in ¼ cup flour and cook until thickened. (Add more marinade if needed to reach desired consistency.)

Spoon marinade gravy over the meat and serve immediately.

Tip: Serve over roasted red potatoes that have been sprinkled with parsley.

OMIE'S FRIED RABBIT

Ingredients

1 rabbit, quartered

Water with 2 T. salt

1 cup all-purpose flour

1 tsp. salt

½ tsp. pepper

1 cup olive or canola cooking oil

Directions

Soak the rabbit pieces in cold saltwater and refrigerate for 1 hour. Remove the rabbit from the water and rinse with cold, clean water.

Parboil the rabbit by putting it in a pot, covering it with water, heating to a boil, and letting it boil for a few minutes. Remove the rabbit from the water and let it cool. Roll the rabbit pieces in flour seasoned with salt and pepper.

In a heavy skillet, heat the olive oil until it's hot. Fry the rabbit until it is crispy.

RABBIT PIE

Ingredients

1 rabbit

Water with 2 T. salt

Pie Shells

2 cups all-purpose flour, sifted

1 tsp. salt

4 T. butter

6 T. shortening (Crisco preferred)

6 T. milk

Filling

1 (10.5 oz.) can mushroom soup

8 oz. chicken broth (or water)

1 (8 oz.) pkg. frozen peas and carrots

2 cups diced potatoes

Salt and pepper to taste

Directions

Cover the rabbit in saltwater and refrigerate overnight. Remove rabbit from saltwater and rinse well in clean water.

Place the rabbit in a Crock-Pot and cook until tender on medium heat. This can take 3 to 4 hours. Don't add salt until meat is cooked (to keep it tender). Cook rabbit until the bones can be removed easily.

Take rabbit out of pot and remove the bones. (This is a good time to double-check that all buckshot is removed). Break into bite-size pieces, put into a pan, and set aside.

Pie Shells

Sift flour and salt together into a medium-size bowl. Cut in shortening and butter with a pastry blender or large fork. Add milk. Gently stir with fork until well mixed. Add more flour if needed for desired consistency.

Divide dough in half and form two balls. Place dough balls on a floured surface and roll out each ball until dough is thin and big enough to fit the pie pan.

Place one pastry shell in bottom of pie pan, gently conforming to the pan's shape.

Filling

Preheat oven to 350°. To the meat, add the mushroom soup and broth. Heat thoroughly.

Cook the peas, carrots, and potatoes until tender and drain. Combine the veggies with the meat mixture. Add salt and pepper to taste.

Place all the ingredients in the unbaked pie shell. Cover with the second pie shell and crimp pastry edges together. Brush top with butter.

Bake for 30 minutes.

THERE'S MORE THAN ONE WAY TO BAG A RABBIT

It was December, the year before I (Steve) turned fifteen. My friend Kenny and I were rabbit hunting the brushy banks of a creek in West Virginia. We both had single-shot, 20-gauge shotguns. We held them ready to fire at any cottontail we hoped would appear at any moment.

After an hour of walking and kicking frost-covered clumps of heavy grass, without success of stirring up rabbits, Kenny decided to try the other side of the creek. He found a narrow spot where he thought he could jump from one bank to the other. The bank he was jumping from was higher than the other bank by about five feet. The creek was six or seven feet wide, making it necessary for him to back up to get a running start. He broke his 20-gauge open, ejected and pocketed the shell for safety's sake, and proceeded to make the flying leap.

Being quite the athlete, Kenny had no trouble clearing the water. When he touched down on the other side, he landed on a sizable clump of grass. As his boots connected with the earth, I heard an unusual squeal. I thought he'd knocked the wind out of himself or maybe sprained an ankle. Then I heard him yell, "Did you hear that?"

"Yeah! You okay?" I asked.

Kenny laughed. "Yeah, I'm okay but this big rabbit ain't doin' so good!"

My friend had landed squarely on one of the biggest rabbits we'd ever seen. The impact killed it outright. Its hiding place in the heavy grass was an unfortunate choice. Kenny had done something that only one in a million—make that one in two million—could do. He'd killed a rabbit with his boots. He proved there's more than one way to bag a cottontail. As it turned out, it was the only catch of the day.

BAKED WABBIT

SUBMITTED BY EVELYN BLEDSOE

Ingredients

2 T. solid shortening

1 or 2 large rabbits, cut into pieces

½ cup all-purpose flour

2 cups water

Salt and pepper

Directions

Melt shortening in a large, iron skillet. Roll the rabbit pieces in flour and place in the skillet. Brown on both sides. Remove the rabbit pieces and place them in a single layer in a small roasting pan. Season with salt and pepper.

Pour drippings from the skillet into the roasting pan. Add the water. Cover the pan with a tight-fitting lid or place foil securely on top of the pan.

Bake for 2 hours at 350°.

Tip: Serve the rabbit hot along with Poor Man's Gravy (page 186) made with the drippings.

RABBIT ON THE RIVER

BY ALICE CLICK (ANNIE'S SISTER)

During rabbit season in the 1960s, Dad would load us kids into his old, one-ton truck that could go just about anywhere. He'd take us to the part of our property he called "The Kanawha River Bottom Farm." He would get into the back of the truck and hold the shotgun on the cab roof. Mother would drive around in the field, and before too long we kids would see a rabbit—sometimes several—highlighted by the headlights of the truck. Dad would take aim the best he could. BANG went the shotgun. He would jump down from the truck bed, retrieve the rabbit, and place it in a coffee sack.

Mother would drive around the field a few more times. Usually Dad would have bagged a half dozen rabbits before the evening was over. These rabbits were plump from feeding on Daddy's crops. Arriving home with a truckload of sleepy kids, they would put us to bed and then the real work began. Mom and Dad butchered the rabbits. It would be midnight before they finished the messy job and put the meat into the freezer.

Admittedly, we kids never considered the legality of Dad's rabbit hunting method, but we know his heart was in the right place. He was feeding his family and ridding his farm of crop moochers. As kids, our only concern was how soon we would get to enjoy what Mom would do with those soon-to-be-yummy bunnies.

When it was time to cook the rabbits, Mom would thaw the meat and make her famous "Rabbit and Gravy" meal (recipe on the next page.)

ROASTED RABBIT

Ingredients

1 rabbit

2 T. lemon juice

1 tsp. onion powder

1 tsp. garlic powder

Nonstick cooking oil

3 T. butter, melted

Directions

Rub the surface of the rabbit meat with lemon juice, onion powder, and garlic powder.

Place meat on a greased rack in a shallow pan. Brush meat generously with melted butter. Cover loosely with foil or, if you prefer, place the rabbit in a well-greased roaster pan with lid.

Roast at 325° for 2½ hours or until desired doneness.

MAMA'S RABBIT AND GRAVY

Ingredients

1 rabbit

Water with a dash of salt

1½ cups flour, divided

Salt and pepper

¼ cup cooking oil

Directions

Cut the rabbit into pieces by separating it at the joints. Soak the meat in the cold saltwater. Let it soak for a couple of hours if possible.

Put the rabbit in a fresh pan of water and bring to a slow boil. Remove rabbit and drain, saving the "rabbit broth."

Roll the pieces of rabbit in ½ cup of flour and season with salt and pepper. Heat the oil in a cast-iron skillet and add rabbit. Fry until meat is tender and cooked all the way through. Remove the rabbit and set aside.

Add 1 cup of flour to the oil in the skillet and stir, making sure it doesn't burn. Pour the rabbit broth into the skillet. Turn down the temperature, cook, and stir until mixture reaches gravy consistency.

Pour gravy over rabbit and serve.

Tip: Serve with mashed potatoes and Sylvie Biscuits (page 163).

RABBIT NORMANDY

Ingredients

2 eggs

½ cup milk

½ cup flour

½ cup cornmeal

2 rabbits, cut into pieces

Salt and pepper

¾ cup bacon grease
    (or vegetable oil)

1 shallot (or onion), chopped

2 cups apple cider

Directions

Beat eggs and milk in a bowl, and then pour into a shallow dish.

Put flour in one pie tin and put cornmeal in another pie tin. Dip sections of rabbit in egg mixture, then flour, then cornmeal, and place on a plate. Season meat with salt and pepper. Let set for 10 to 15 minutes.

In a large skillet, melt bacon grease over low flame. Brown the shallot and then remove it (the onion flavor is now in the oil).

Sauté the rabbit in bacon grease until well done. Reduce flame and pour the apple cider over the rabbit. Cover the skillet and simmer very slowly until liquid has been absorbed or evaporated.

Part Three

FOWL

Turkey

 **TIPS FOR COOKING GAME BIRDS**

The flavor and quality of the dining experience when it comes to wild game birds is largely determined by the care given by the hunter after bagging the bird. Here are some suggestions to be assured of the best taste when cooking.

• Wild turkey should be bled and cleaned immediately after shooting. Be sure to remove the oil sacs at the base of the back near the tail.

• Double-check the meat for bullets, shot, or pellets. Use your fingertips to detect any shot that might have fragmented during the kill.

• Keep the meat cool until cooking. If desired, freeze the birds while they are fresh and in top condition using materials designed for keeping meat properly frozen. Remove as much air as possible from the bird meat package when sealing for the freezer. Keep meat at 0° or lower. Make sure you use meat within six months of freezing.

• Before cooking, trim off all fat.

• Dry cooking methods, such as frying, grilling, and broiling, are good for young birds.

• Moist cooking methods, such as stewing, baking, and braising, are best for older birds.

• To prevent skinned or older birds from drying out during baking, wrap each piece with a strip of bacon. The age of the wild turkey makes a difference in cooking preparations. The way to determine age is in the length of its spurs. Located on the inside of the legs about 3½ inches above the feet, young birds have short, dull spurs while older birds have long, sharp spurs. The older the bird, the tougher the meat. When cooking an older turkey, sprinkle commercial tenderizer in the body cavity and refrigerate for 12 to 24 hours.

I LOVE THE WILD TURKEY!

I'll (Steve) never forget the first time I stood at the microphone as a keynote speaker at a church-sponsored wild game dinner. I said, "I love wild turkey!" When I said it, I heard some gasps in the room. I wasn't sure why, and I paused for about two seconds to process the unexpected reaction. Then I suddenly realized there is a potent whiskey on the market called Wild Turkey. Convinced that there were those in the room who might be familiar with the "golden fire water," I immediately attempted to halt any fears and potential rumors.

"Let me rephrase my statement: I love the wild turkey—the bird!" I was relieved to hear laughter. And since it garnered such a response, I've been guilty of using that same line at events where hunters are present. I do it for the chuckle and to get a feel for my audience.

Seriously, I really enjoy chasing turkeys—big time! If you were to ask me which I like better — deer or turkey hunting —I would reply, "They're both on the same line." But in the category of which critter requires the least effort to get it home, the turkey wins—wings down. And if you were to ask which is easier to process, then I'd guess you've never killed a deer and a turkey. It takes about ten minutes to properly remove the edible meat from a turkey compared to upwards of two hours to field dress a deer (at least the way I do it).

While the yield of venison is worth the work (in Tennessee the outcome is, on average, 35 to 55 pounds of meat), an average turkey in our area might yield two to four pounds of meat. Though much less in yield, turkey is just as exciting to cook and tasty to consume.

The following recipes are not only delicious, they also provide a way of honoring the legacy of wild turkey...the bird, that is.

"GOBBLE IT UP" WILD TURKEY

Ingredients

6 cups diced cooked turkey breast

3 cups breadcrumbs

¾ cup chopped celery

1 onion, chopped

½ cup butter

½ tsp. poultry seasoning

1 egg, beaten

¾ cup milk

1 (10.5 oz.) can cream of
  mushroom soup

Directions

Preheat oven to 350°. Place turkey in a 9 x 13-inch rectangular baking pan.

In a skillet, sauté breadcrumbs, celery, and onion in butter. Add poultry seasoning, egg, and milk. Spoon the mixture over the turkey. Pour and spread mushroom soup over the top.

Bake uncovered for 45 minutes.

THE DOUBLE TAKE

A joyful heart is good medicine" (Proverbs 17:22). When I (Steve) hunt with my friend Don Hicks, I usually leave with my heart light and my soul nurtured. Why? Because we seem to do more laughing than hunting. And believe me, we do a lot of hunting at his place. While every visit is memorable, one of the best involves a spring gobbler hunt in a small pop-up blind best occupied by one person—but we were both crammed inside.

Sunrise came around six thirty, and by eight we already experienced a morning of out-of-control laughter at everything from how pitiful our turkey-calling skills were to the silly twists we put on the old songs we were singing. Our sides were aching as we amused ourselves while trying hard to keep the hilarity down to a low roar.

Then Don took a look outside, and his eyes got bigger than fried turkey eggs. He pointed out the small window. "Steve, there's a huge gobbler right in front of us. Take it!"

We scrambled to put on ear protection. The unexpected, out of nowhere appearance of the big bird brought on some major pre-shot jitters for me. As if the abrupt chaos inside the tiny tent was not enough to challenge my attempt to hold my shotgun steady, Don suddenly slipped off his little stool, dropped to his knees on the grass inside the blind, and curled up tightly in a strange position. I had no idea what he was doing, but it sure looked like he was praying. I knew if I laughed like I wanted to at the sight of this supposed intercessory moment on his part, I'd never close the deal on the gobbler. So I focused on putting the bead on the bird. (I found out later Don wasn't interceding at all. He was trying to make room for me to maneuver my 12-gauge to the little window so I could take the shot.)

When I pulled the trigger, the concussion from the heavily loaded 3½-inch shell nearly threw the lightweight blind off of us. Before the report of the shot faded to silence, Don was up on his knees looking out the window to see if I'd connected. When he looked, his eyes widened again. He whispered excitedly, "There's another bird out there! Where's my gun?"

As he scrambled for his gun, I quickly peeked out the window. Sure enough, there was a second nervous gobbler going in circles around his friend who had, as far as he was concerned, suddenly exploded. I figured the second bird was saying, "Dude, if that's what springtime love does to a feller, you can count me out!"

Unfortunately for the lingering gobbler, while his attention was focused on his friend, he didn't notice the two of us shifting around inside the blind. Undoubtedly we looked like Houdini trying to escape from a huge canvas sack. If the bird had noticed, he could have made a lifesaving exit from the area. However, he stayed around long enough for Don to stick the barrel of his gun out the window and touch off a shot. And when Don pulled the trigger, I was on my knees inside the tent wadded up in the prayer position.

Within twenty seconds of the first shot fired, we had two birds outside the tent. With our kills separated by such a small number of seconds, we both agreed that this qualified as a "double kill." After a very, very short pause, filled with us staring at each other in awe at what had just happened, we broke into full-volume frivolity and unrestrained congratulations.

What a huge relief to be able to open up with our laughter. We'd spent the morning trying so hard to suppress our noise that we were worried we'd be going into cardiac arrest. As we lifted the super-lightweight blind off us and cast it aside, we stood unhidden before our feathered targets. They were still doing the death dance that happens after birds are killed, which told us we needed to hurry over and pin them down. Without hesitation, we took off toward the birds.

Both gobblers were about the same size, and there wasn't a way to tell which of us shot which bird, but it didn't matter. We knew they were big enough specimens that when laid side-by-side, the double take would get a double take from all onlookers. We couldn't wait to get them home and sit down to a tasty reward for our morning's work.

Doris Hicks, Don's sweet wife, knows how to turn a double take into a delicious dinner. You'll enjoy her recipe for turkey medallions!

DORIS'S FRIED TURKEY MEDALLIONS

Ingredients

1 wild turkey breast

½ cup flour

½ tsp. cayenne pepper

Herbs de Provence mix*

Salt and pepper

¼ cup cooking oil

Honey mustard (or other dipping sauce, see page 194)

*To make your own Herbs de Provence mix, combine these dried herbs:

3 T. marjoram

3 T. thyme

3 T. summer savory

1 T. lavender

1 tsp. basil

1 tsp. rosemary

½ tsp. sage

½ tsp. fennel seeds

Directions

Cut the turkey breast into 2-inch wide sections. (The yield for each side of an average turkey breast will be approximately two 8-inch sections).

Roll the sections inside wax paper and freeze until almost solid to make for easy slicing. Cut the cooled sections of turkey into ½-inch slices (should yield 16 to 20 medallions).

Mix flour and cayenne pepper together.

Rub turkey with Herbs de Provence, roll meat in flour and cayenne mix, and season with salt and pepper.

Fry in cooking oil until lightly brown.

Serve hot with honey mustard for dipping.

TURKEY DRESSING CASSEROLE

Ingredients

1 turkey breast

1 medium onion, chopped

2 ribs celery, chopped

1 (10.5 oz.) can cream of mushroom soup

4 oz. milk

1 (8 oz.) container sour cream

Nonstick cooking spray

1 (12 oz.) pkg. dry stuffing

Directions

In a large pot of water, cook the turkey breast, onion, and celery until tender.

Remove turkey from liquid (this will be your broth) and cut into chunks. Reserve the broth: strain into a large bowl and set aside the onion and celery for the stuffing.

Preheat oven to 350°.

In a separate bowl, mix the soup, milk, and sour cream. Add the turkey and stir.

Pour the meat mixture into a greased casserole dish.

Prepare the stuffing according to package directions.

Add reserved onion and celery to the stuffing and spread over the turkey mixture.

Bake for 30 minutes or until the dish is bubbling and the stuffing is brown.

ANNIE'S GOLD NUGGET WILD TURKEY

Ingredients

1 turkey breast

1 cup flour

1 tsp. salt

½ tsp. pepper

1 tsp. garlic powder

½ tsp. paprika

3 T. cooking oil (or butter)

Directions

Cut the turkey breast into 1-inch nuggets.

Combine flour, salt, pepper, garlic powder, and paprika. Dredge the turkey nuggets in the flour mixture.

Pour oil into a heavy skillet and heat to medium-hot. (If you use butter, which tastes yummy, make sure the temperature is not so hot that the butter burns.) Fry the nuggets until golden brown. Remove meat from skillet and place on a paper towel to drain excess oil.

Tip: Serve with Mom's Morel Mushrooms (page 158) and Homemade Dipping Sauce (page 194).

WILD TURKEY CROCK-POT SUPPER

Ingredients

1 large turkey breast

3 cups chicken broth (or water)

1 (15 oz.) can cream of mushroom soup

1 (15 oz.) can cream of celery soup

Salt and pepper

Mrs. Dash original seasoning

Directions

Place the turkey breast in a Crock-Pot. Add chicken broth and simmer on low for 2 hours.

Add mushroom and celery soup and continue to cook on low for 2 hours.

Add seasonings and, if needed, more water or broth to keep meat covered. Cook until tender.

SWEET-AND-SOUR WILD TURKEY WITH RICE

Ingredients

3 T. cooking oil

1½ lbs. turkey breast

1½ cups water

1 (20 oz.) can chunk pineapple
  with juice

¼ cup brown sugar

2 T. cornstarch

¼ cup apple cider vinegar

2 T. soy sauce

½ tsp. kosher salt (kosher salt is purer, doesn't contain additives, and is milder than iodized table salt)

1 green pepper, cut into strips

1 onion, sliced thin

12 oz. rice

Directions

Cut the turkey into ½-inch cubes.

In a heavy skillet, heat the oil and then brown the turkey. (Do not drain the oil.) Add water, cover, and simmer until the meat is tender, about 1 hour.

Drain the chunk pineapple, saving the juice for later.

Combine the brown sugar and cornstarch in a medium saucepan. Add the pineapple juice, apple cider vinegar, soy sauce, and salt. Cook until it starts to boil. Add the turkey meat. Cook until meat is done and sauce thickens, approximately 20 minutes. (If more liquid is needed, add a little bit of water.)

Add the pineapple, green pepper, and onion. Cook 3 to 5 more minutes until the vegetables are at desired tenderness.

Prepare rice according to package instructions.

Serve turkey over rice.

EMMITT'S FIRST TURKEY

When Emmitt Beall joined our family in the year 2000 by marrying our daughter, Heidi, there were several things I (Steve) immediately liked about the young man. Mostly, I liked that we had a lot in common. He's handsome, athletic, very intelligent, and a hard worker. (Okay, maybe we only have a few things in common...) People say girls grow up and marry men just like their daddies, which may be why mothers cry at weddings.

There was another thing I liked about Emmitt that I learned about later. Something Emmitt didn't even know when he got hitched to Heidi—but he certainly knows it now. He's a born hunter. And I'm happy to report that I helped him make the discovery! It happened one joyful spring when I suggested Emmitt join me for a gobbler hunt.

With his borrowed camo clothes, boots, and my old pump-action, 12-gauge Remington, Emmitt was ready to go. We arrived at the farm where we would hunt about 30 minutes before daylight. I set us up at the edge of a long field where I hoped turkeys would show up. Sure enough, about an hour after daylight we heard gobbling at the upper end of the field. A group of hens and bearded toms were coming our way. It wouldn't be too long before the boys in the flock would see my attractive hen decoy placed approximately fifteen yards from us.

Believing the birds would appear over a little rise to our left, I instructed Emmitt to position his gun at a ninety degree angle from the decoy and put his finger lightly on the safety, ready to push it to the off position. But the birds fooled me.

Three gobblers decided to go around the little rise. That surprise put Emmitt in a predicament. To attempt a shot, he had to swing his gun to the right. I was sure a newbie hunter wouldn't be able to accomplish such a feat with three pairs of turkey eyes (and their keen vision) only twenty or so yards away. However, I noticed the birds were focused on the fake hen, so I quietly whispered to Emmitt, "If you think you can move as slow as a shadow on a sundial to get your gun around to one of those birds, go ahead and try it!"

What I saw next will always be one of the most amazing moments I've enjoyed while chasing turkeys. Emmitt began an incredibly slow and deliberate movement of his gun while releasing the safety. After at least a minute and a half of steady and sure maneuvering, he drew a bead on one of the birds and pulled the trigger. The gobbler hit the ground. Emmitt jumped up and ran to his well-earned trophy.

I couldn't believe what I'd just seen. A first-timer had pulled off what many of us old-timers are still trying to do. How he managed to move so slowly with minimal noise, I'll never know. That day I knew my daughter had married a natural hunter.

Like I said, people say girls grow up and marry men just like their daddies...and that's why dads smile at weddings!

LESSONS FROM THE "CONCESSION" STAND

Spring turkey season was in full swing in Tennessee. Because I (Steve) rarely pass up a chance to chase some birds, when my buddy Lindsey Williams called and asked if I wanted to join him the next morning for a hunt in his "Concession" stand (where we hide, eat, drink coffee, and wait for critters to show up), I answered yes before he could utter the last word of the invite. Before you start looking for a way to express your pity for my addiction to the chase, please understand that, for me, hunting is more than just providing meat for the table. There is an even more redeemable element to my obsession.

When I go hunting, it is also research. Each trip is an adventure into fields of truth from the Lord. I receive myriad insights for my own discovery and book research: insights about relationships with God, with others, and about His creation. My hunt with Lindsey provides a good example of what can be discovered out there if a person is on the lookout.

About thirty minutes after daylight, Lindsey and I saw a hen wander into the huge meadow we were watching. She was about 200 yards from us. A minute or so later, we caught sight of two adult toms entering the field near the hen. Lindsey and I smiled as we silently encouraged the hen to move across the field toward us as she fed. However, it seemed she was about to lead the two gobblers away... but suddenly the two boys looked across the field in our direction and the game changed. What they saw was too much for their bird brains to resist.

Lindsey has a decoy called B-Mobile. It's a life-size strutting turkey that is painted in vivid detail. It sports a real turkey fan mounted in full bloom. Next to B-Mobile, Lindsey had placed a hen decoy in a position that indicated it was receptive to breeding. When the two amorous male birds caught sight of another male in full strut and about to close the deal with a hen, jealousy and desire took over.

The two mature gobblers did something that was actually out of character for birds their age. They turned their attention away from the hen in front of them and made their way across the field toward the two decoys. They left the real thing alone, leaving her bewildered, offended, and miffed. Within a minute or so, the two lovesick and dangerously jealous gobblers closed in on B-Mobile. When they got closer, they completely lost control of their emotions. Both of them gobbled simultaneously, loudly to say the least, and forcefully enough that we nearly felt the wind from their angry rant. We're not sure what they said, but whatever it was, it would be their last words.

They proceeded to show fight as they neared and made several wide circles around B-Mobile. Just as they were about to attack their plastic counterpart, I heard Lindsey softly give the count-up. "One, two, three..." At three, the field rumbled with the report of two 12-gauge weapons of destruction. Instantly two toms paid a huge price for succumbing to jealous and covetous rage.

What was the takeaway from the field besides some really good eats? The obvious lesson gleaned from the two deceased birds is that a man should never ignore the deadly danger of yielding to jealousy. He should always heed the warning found in commandment number ten: "You shall not covet your neighbor's wife" (Deuteronomy 5:21). It's not a safe thing to do!

Blessings on your hunting and research. Each time you go, may you too find meat for your body and soul.

POACHED TURKEY BREAST

Ingredients

1 skinless wild turkey breast, rinsed and patted dry

1 large onion, chopped

3 carrots, chopped

2 bay leaves

2 T. salt

1 tsp. whole black peppercorns

6 T. distilled white vinegar

Poached turkey doesn't mean stealing one from your neighbor's land. Nope. We're talking a good way to prepare a turkey breast for eating or to use in other recipes.

Directions

To determine ideal amount of liquid needed for poaching, put turkey breast in a deep pot and add enough cold water to cover by 1 inch. Now remove the turkey, leaving the water in the pot.

Put onion, carrot, bay leaves, salt, peppercorns, and vinegar in the pot. Bring to a boil.

Carefully put turkey breast into pot to avoid splashing. Reduce heat to a bare simmer.

Cook covered for 1¼ hours.

Remove from heat and let turkey cool in the liquid, uncovered, for 30 minutes. Drain and discard solids.

Serve cold or at room temperature.

LEMON MARINATED WILD TURKEY BREAST

Ingredients

1 poached wild turkey breast (see
    Poached Turkey Breast, page 112)

1 lemon

⅓ cup golden raisins

3 T. fresh lemon juice

1½ tsp. balsamic vinegar

1 tsp. salt

½ cup olive oil

2 T. capers, drained

3 T. pine nuts

1 T. chopped fresh parsley

1 T. chopped fresh mint

Directions

Place poached turkey in a ziplock bag.

Carefully peel lemon, being careful to avoid the white part of the rind, which is extremely bitter. Cut peel into ½-inch strips and set aside.

Soak raisins in boiling water for 5 minutes. Drain and set aside.

In a small bowl, whisk lemon juice, balsamic vinegar, and salt together. Gradually pour olive oil into mixture, whisking to emulsify (thicken). Stir in lemon zest strips, raisins, and capers.

Pour liquid mixture into ziplock bag with turkey. Marinate in the refrigerator for 4 hours or overnight.

Toast pine nuts by placing them in a dry skillet. Cook on medium heat until nuts are brown, stirring constantly. Set aside.

Remove turkey from marinade, setting the liquid aside. Cut turkey breast, on the diagonal, into ¼-inch strips.

Stir parsley and mint into marinade.

Place turkey on serving plate and spoon marinade dressing over meat. Sprinkle with toasted pine nuts. Serve cold or at room temperature.

Quail

 **COOKING TIPS FOR QUAIL**

- Serving size: Allow 1 to 2 quail per person

- Be careful not to overcook quail meat. It will become dry and tough. When is quail cooked properly? When the meat is slightly firm to the touch, similar to cooked chicken breast, and when the juices are clear.

- To determine whether a game bird is young and tender, the answer is as close as its bill. The stiffness of the bill is usually a good indicator. Lift the bird by its lower jaw. If nothing breaks, it's probably a mature bird. Because older birds tend to not be as tender as younger ones, you may need to adjust the recipe by marinating and cooking the meat a bit longer. Or you might choose a moist cooking method, such as stewing, baking, or braising.

GRILLED QUAIL

Ingredients

4 quail

Marinade (See "Gravies, Marinades, and Sauces," page 185, or try Newman's Own Marinade)

Nonstick cooking spray

Directions

Place quail in a large ziplock bag. Add enough marinade to cover meat. Refrigerate for at least 8 hours, turning occasionally.

Coat the grill with nonstick cooking spray. Grill quail for 15 minutes per side, basting with the marinade.

LEAVELL QUAIL WITH RICE AND GRAVY

Ingredients

20 quail, ready to cook

½ cup Cavender's All-purpose Greek Seasoning

1 cup all-purpose flour, divided

½ cup canola oil

⅛ cup water

1 cup milk

Salt and pepper to taste

1 box instant brown rice

Directions

Season both sides of the quail liberally with Cavender's seasoning.

Dredge quail in ½ cup of flour and place in a large iron skillet with hot canola oil ⅛-inch deep. Cook until brown, 2 to 3 minutes. Flip the quail and brown other side. Do not drain skillet.

Turn heat to low. Add ⅛ cup of water, cover loosely, and simmer, steaming the meat until tender. Remove quail to a warming plate.

Loosen drippings from the bottom of the pan. Add oil if more liquid needed and heat until hot. Add ½ cup flour and stir, cooking until brown. Add milk, stirring constantly. When consistency is like gravy, remove from heat. Salt and pepper to taste.

Prepare rice according to package instructions.

Serve quail and gravy over the brown rice.

FRIED QUAIL

Ingredients

3 cups buttermilk, divided

2 T. seasoning salt

2 T. hot sauce

1 T. minced garlic

8 quail, whole

2 cups all-purpose flour

Peanut oil

Directions

In a large bowl, combine half the buttermilk with your favorite seasoning salt, hot sauce, and garlic. Mix thoroughly.

Add quail to buttermilk mixture and refrigerate for 4 to 24 hours.

Put flour in a ziplock bag. Dredge quail in the flour a few pieces at a time.

In a separate bowl, pour the remaining buttermilk. Dip the floured pieces of quail into the buttermilk. Once again, dredge the quail pieces in the flour. Place the coated pieces on a rack and allow to rest for 5 to 10 minutes.

In a large, heavy pot, heat peanut oil that is 4 inches deep to a temperature of 325°. Gently add quail (to avoid splatter). Fry until meat is golden brown and floats to the top of the oil. This should take 5 to 8 minutes.

Allow cooked quail to drain on paper towels before serving.

Tip: Serve with Three Corn Casserole (page 152).

QUAIL WITH CHITTERLINGS

Ingredients

2 quail (including intestines, liver, gizzard)

Salt and pepper

½ cup chopped onion

3 T. bacon drippings
(or 3 T. cooking oil)

Directions

Take the chitterlings (intestines) of two fat, full-grown quail and empty them of their contents under running water. Open them with a sharp knife and scrape off the inner coat. Wash them carefully.

Boil the chitterlings with the liver and gizzard. Season with salt and pepper. Add onion. When meats are tender, set them aside to cool.

Put some bacon drippings into a skillet and fry the quail to a nice brown.

Tip: Serve with Poor Man's Gravy (page 186). This recipe also works with other types of fowl.

Pheasant

When the plane landed in Des Moines, Iowa, my son, Nathan, and his friend Joey were giddy with anticipation for the hunt we were about to enjoy. I (Steve) was just as excited. It was our first-ever pheasant hunt. And to top it off, we had a personal guide—a local farmer who owned a great bird dog. We were pumped!

By midafternoon, our host was parking his truck along a paved country road near his farm and opening the doors for us and his fine pointer. We grabbed our trio of 12-gauge shotguns, loaded them, and were ready to head into the field with our new friend. But before we left the truck, we received some important instructions from our host.

"Guys, I can't tell you how glad I am that you're here. I've looked forward to showing you a good time. I know this is your first pheasant hunt, so I have to let you in on some rules of the game."

We didn't utter a sound as our tutor continued.

"There are just three things I want you to remember. First, don't take a shot unless you first quickly check to make sure humans are not standing beyond your barrel. I don't want to be interrupting our hunt with yanking buckshot out of somebody. Two, be mindful of where the dog is at all times—especially when you pull the trigger. A dead dog can end a lively hunt real quick. Third, if you hear me say 'hen,' don't you dare pull the trigger. We can't shoot hens here in Iowa, and if somebody happened to see us do it, I'd be in a heap of trouble."

He paused and looked at each one of us. "You boys got all that?"

Like good soldiers we barked a respectful, "Yes, sir!" And with that we were on our way into the field to hunt rooster pheasants.

The orange-and-white Brittany was totally engaged in the hunt and ran around like he was happy to be alive. Nathan, Joey, and I had our shotguns resting on our hips as we walked side-by-side about twenty-five yards apart, ready for the first pheasant to fly up. Suddenly, right between Nathan and Joey, a bird lifted off. The whoofing of the wings was a unique and rather loud announcement that a bird was ascending. Then we heard a yell from our host: "Hit it!"

With that command, Joey threw his gun up to his shoulder, pointed it in the direction of the flying feast, and pulled the trigger. Instantly the pheasant folded its wings and crashed to the earth about thirty yards from us. We three hunters were laughing and smiling, but our joy quickly turned to horror when we realized our host was marching toward us with a livid look on his face.

"Boys! We're right here by a road, and you killed a hen. I was sure I said you can't kill a hen! Didn't you hear me say 'hen'?"

The three of us looked at each other. Our expressions said what we were all thinking, but Joey vocalized our thoughts: "Sir, didn't you say 'Hit it'?"

That's exactly what I thought I'd heard, and I was sure Nathan heard that too. But boy were we wrong!

"No, son," the farmer said. "I said 'hen'!"

Joey then politely asked a question that didn't elicit a timid answer. "Is there any way you can say something else? Like 'Don't shoot—it's a hen?'"

Our host's response didn't get a challenge from us. "Boys, for more than thirty years I've been saying 'hen' when it's a hen, and I ain't changing things now. You're just gonna have to listen better."

I'm happy to report that not one more illegal bird fell to the ground on that trip. And we managed to take several legal birds. Even more important, each one of us took something home from Iowa that we still use to this day. The three of us are better listeners!

Tip: Typically, one pheasant will feed three people.

SLOW-COOKER PHEASANT OVER RICE

Ingredients

2 T. olive oil

2 garlic cloves, minced

¼ cup onion

1 pheasant, cut into small pieces
   (or 3 lbs. of small birds)

1 cup chicken broth

2 T. brown sugar

½ T. poultry seasoning

1 tsp. salt

1 tsp. pepper

½ cup sour cream

2 T. flour

1 cup milk

12 oz. rice

Directions

Put olive oil in a large skillet and heat. Sauté garlic and onion until they are transparent. Remove garlic and onion, leaving the oil.

Brown the meat pieces in the oil. Add the garlic and onion.

In a separate bowl, mix the chicken broth, brown sugar, and seasonings. Pour over the meat and heat thoroughly.

Pour skillet contents into a slow cooker. Cook on high until the bird is tender and falls off the bone, approximately 3½ hours.

Remove the bird, debone, and set meat aside.

Put the sour cream, flour, and milk into the liquid in the slow cooker and stir. Add the meat, and cook on low until broth is thick, approximately 1 hour.

Prepare rice according to package instructions.

Serve pheasant on a bed of rice.

CRISPY PHEASANT

Ingredients

2 pheasants, butterfly cut

3 T. butter or margarine

Salt and pepper

¼ lb. bacon, cut in strips

Directions

Rub the pheasants with butter and then season with salt and pepper.

Put the birds in a buttered casserole dish. Place the bacon on top of the birds.

Bake at 400° for 1 hour or until crispy and golden brown, basting with the buttery juices often.

Duck

 **DUCK COOKING TIPS**

- Ducks and geese should be plucked rather than skinned to retain flavor and moisture during cooking.

- Some people think waterfowl meat tastes best when it is aged. To age, hang the duck in a cool, dry area for 24 to 48 hours before cutting up. Try it and see how you like it. Check online for more ideas, suggestions, and instructions for aging meat.

- Older ducks and geese can be marinated in a solution of ½ teaspoon salt and 1 tablespoon vinegar per quart of cold water for 4 to 12 hours in the refrigerator. You may want to skin those birds that have had a diet of aquatic vegetation and animals.

- Fish-eating ducks (those with pointed or serrated bills) are best marinated before cooking. Use a marinade high in acid, such as lemon, lime juice, vinegar, wine, or buttermilk to remove any fishy or gamy taste.

- In the fall, ducks have a more desirable flavor than at other times of the year. If you are put off by the strong game flavor of some ducks, try soaking the meat in a bath of fairly strong salt water with a teaspoon of baking soda for a few days. Freezing a bird for a week or two will also help tenderize it.

PAN-FRIED DUCK BREAST NUGGETS

Ingredients

4 duck breasts, cut into 1-inch strips

1½ cups water with 2 tsp. salt

1 cup all-purpose flour

½ cup canola cooking oil

2 T. butter

2 tsp. dry steak seasoning

Salt and pepper

Dipping sauces (see Gravies, Marinades, and Sauces, page 185)

Directions

Marinate the duck breast in saltwater for 36 to 48 hours. Remove from marinade and pat dry with paper towel.

Dredge duck in flour.

In a heavy skillet, combine the cooking oil and butter using medium heat. Fry the duck meat 3 to 5 minutes on each side, cooking to medium rare or desired doneness. (Do not overcook or meat will dry out.) Season with salt, pepper, and steak seasoning.

Serve immediately with dipping sauce.

GRILLED DUCK BREAST SALAD

Ingredients

3 to 4 duck breasts

Marinade

¾ cup Italian salad dressing

¼ cup Dale's Seasoning

Salad

2 T. butter

1 cup pecans, chopped

1 head romaine lettuce, washed, broken into pieces

1 cup sweetened, dried cranberries (or Craisins)

1 cup Sweet-and-Sour Sauce (page 193)

Directions

Put the duck pieces in a large ziplock bag.

Mix the Italian dressing and Dale's Seasoning. Pour into bag of duck breasts and marinate overnight in the refrigerator.

Remove duck breasts from marinade and grill over medium-hot fire, 4 minutes per side. (Do not overcook.) Meat should be a little pink in the center when done.

Chill the meat in the refrigerator until thoroughly cooled.

Thinly slice duck breast and set aside.

Melt butter in a skillet. Add pecans and cook until toasted, approximately 2½ minutes. Remove pecans from skillet and place on paper towels to drain and sit until cool to the touch.

In a large bowl, toss the lettuce, cranberries, and pecans.

Lay slices of grilled duck on top of the greens. Pour sweet-and-sour sauce over everything and serve.

DUCK GUMBO

Ingredients

3 ducks

1 chicken breast

1 lb. smoked sausage, chopped

2 bunches green onions, diced

1 bell pepper, chopped

6 ribs celery, chopped

½ cup flour

1 (1.25 oz.) packet Creole gumbo mix

½ tsp. salt

½ tsp. pepper

¼ tsp. cayenne pepper

6 oz. okra, chopped

1 (12 oz.) pkg. rice

1 T. Filé (powdered seasoning)

Our friend LaBreeska Hemphill provided this delicious recipe. When she sent this to us, she also included this note:

"I love to fish. I have a few big-finned trophies on the wall alongside my husband Joel's trophy catches. I've reeled in several large bass out of Lake Guerrero in Mexico. But being married to a hunter and living in Louisiana, I've learned to cook big and small game. Of all the meals I do with wild game, duck gumbo is my favorite. I've made it often when we've had gatherings at the house, and it hits the bull's-eye every time."

Directions

In a very large pot or kettle, boil duck and chicken meat until done. Let cool and remove skin and bones. Put the meat back into the liquid (stock).

In an iron skillet, brown the sausage and drain. Add to stock.

Sauté onion, bell pepper, and celery in sausage drippings. Add to stock, keeping some of the oil in the skillet.

Add flour to the remaining sausage drippings in skillet and brown. Add to stock.

Add Creole seasoning, salt, pepper, and cayenne pepper to stock.

Add okra and bring to a boil.

Prepare rice according to package instructions.

Add Filé to the stock just before serving, stirring very little.

Serve the duck over the hot rice.

Dove

LET DOVE SEASON BEGIN!

For the hunters in our state of Tennessee, as well as many other states in our region of the country, September first is considered a red-letter day. Typically, it's on or about that date when dove season starts. Why is this so special? Very simply, most of us have spent a long summer separated from the fair chase by the laws that govern our legal right to harvest game. Because turkey season ends in early May, we're clawing at the ground to get outdoors to hunt by the time dove season arrives.

Evidence of our excitement and hunger for the hunt can be seen and heard on farms with fields where doves live, eat, and roost. Hunters by the thousands go to the fields early that first morning. Encompassing all ages, men and women take their seats on portable stools and lock and load their weapons.

I've (Steve) been on my share of dove hunts, and usually the more popular dove hot spots are crowded with hunters. We sit within a few yards of each other and blast away at the speedy birds that seem to fly by as fast as a small Cessna. Because they are such tiny targets and hard to bring down, their quick flight down the field creates a sight and sound that is most unique. Like a human wave that a crowd makes in the stands of a football stadium, shooters raise their guns in succession to take their turns at the birds that jet by.

I'm amazed at how many birds get to the end of a field unharmed. Of course, there are a few hunters who are crack shots and bring a halt to the wave moving down the field. However, most of the hunters are like me. When it comes to dove hunting, I estimate we average about a dozen shells per bird.

When the doves aren't flying, most of us are digging into our camo coolers for soft drinks and ham sandwiches. And just about the time we take a first bite of salty ham on white bread lathered with mayo and graced with a juicy late-season tomato, someone yells, "Birds!" We toss down our food, grab our guns, and throw more buckshot. Once that section of the flock has made its way past us, we go back to shoving food into our mouths.

I might not have a lot of success at a dove field, but you can be sure that I have a silo full of fun. And the only thing better than a day of blasting at doves is eating them. Here are a couple of good recipes to help make the expense of all those shotgun shells worth the investment.

DOVE CASSEROLE

Ingredients

6 doves

1 tsp. salt

½ tsp. pepper

2 T. butter

1 small onion, sliced

1 clove garlic, minced

1 bay leaf

2 cups chicken broth

¼ cup shortening (or vegetable oil)

1 T. self-rising flour

8 oz. mushrooms, sliced and sautéed

2 T. ketchup

2 T. sherry (optional)

12 oz. wild rice

Directions

Preheat oven to 350°. Rub the doves with salt, pepper, and butter. Place in a large casserole dish, along with the onion, garlic, bay leaf, and chicken broth.

Cover and bake until meat is tender, approximately 40 minutes. Remove birds from oven and casserole dish.

Melt fat in skillet on medium heat. Blend in flour. Slowly add liquid from casserole dish, stirring constantly. When liquid is thick, add mushrooms, ketchup, and sherry. Simmer a few minutes longer, allowing the flavors to mingle.

Prepare rice according to package instructions.

Serve doves over wild rice.

DOVE STROGANOFF

Ingredients

16 to 18 dove breasts, skin removed

1 medium onion, chopped

3 T. butter

1 (10.5 oz.) can cream of celery soup

1 (6 oz.) can mushroom pieces

½ cup white cooking wine or
   chicken broth

¼ tsp. oregano

¼ tsp. rosemary

1 cup sour cream

1 (12 oz.) pkg. noodles

Directions

Place dove breasts in a large baking dish.

Sauté onion in butter until translucent and put into a large mixing bowl. Add remaining ingredients, except sour cream and noodles, and mix thoroughly. Pour mixture over the doves.

Cover and bake at 350° for approximately 1 hour. Remove from oven, add sour cream, and stir. Return to oven and continue baking, uncovered, for 15 to 20 minutes.

Prepare noodles according to package instructions.

Serve dove mixture over noodles and enjoy!

Chicken

Some serious hunters might wonder why we would include chicken in a cookbook focusing on wild game. Growing up on a farm and among hunters, I have watched the women "hunt down" chickens in the yard and "harvest" them for the dinner table. With homesteading and a seemingly renewed passion for growing healthy, unprocessed meat, raising and roasting chicken is at the top of the list of yummy, chemical-free victuals. Here are some recipes we have enjoyed as well as some from dear friends.

MARY JEAN'S ROASTED CHICKEN

BY MARY JEAN MURPHY

Ingredients

1 (3 to 4 pound) whole fresh chicken

2 T. olive oil

Salt and pepper

Italian seasoning

1 onion, quartered

2 ribs celery, quartered

3 to 4 sprigs fresh rosemary

3 to 4 sprigs fresh thyme

2 T. butter

Directions

Rinse chicken with cold water and pat dry with paper towels. Dry skin ensures crispy skin!

Brush entire chicken with olive oil to lock in moisture and to provide a base for the seasonings to adhere to.

Place in large iron skillet

Generously sprinkle salt, pepper, and Italian seasoning inside and out.

Place quartered onion inside the cavity along with celery, rosemary, thyme, and butter.

Fold wings under to avoid burning the tips.

Roast the chicken uncovered at 425° for approximately 90 minutes (adjust time according to size of the bird) or until golden brown. If skin starts to burn, cover with aluminum foil for the final 10 minutes.

Use a meat thermometer to ensure the meat reaches 165°.

RHODA'S "VERY FRESH" CHICKEN AND DUMPLINGS

BY RHODA GRACE

Ingredients

1 whole raw chicken, plucked and washed with head, feet, and organs removed

Dumplings

1½ cups all-purpose flour
2 tsp. baking powder
¾ tsp. salt
1 T. shortening (lard or Crisco)
¾ cup milk
Dried parsley to taste
Salt and pepper to taste
Onion powder to taste
Garlic powder to taste
Smidge of ground sage

Gravy

½ cup butter
½ cup all-purpose flour
Dried parsley to taste
Salt and pepper to taste
Onion powder to taste
Garlic powder to taste
Smidge of ground sage
Milk and chicken broth, enough to make a nice gravy (about a cup of milk and the rest broth)

Directions

Prepare the Chicken and Broth

Fill medium stock pot half full of water and place whole chicken into the stock pot.

Bring water to boil on high, then reduce to a simmer. Simmer several hours until a nice broth forms. When chicken is cooked to falling off bone, pull the stock pot off the burner.

Debone the chicken and strain out all the bones, skin, etc. Leave all the meat in the stockpot with about 1½ inches of chicken broth. Pour the rest of the chicken broth out into another pan and set aside.

Bring the broth and chicken back to a gentle boil. Make sure that there is a layer of chicken meat that stands out above all the broth. If not, pour more broth out, or pile the chicken meat up on one side of the stockpot so you can place dumplings on top of it.

Make the Dumplings

Whisk all the dry ingredients together in a medium bowl.

Cut the shortening into the dry ingredients.

Add milk and fluff the dough with a fork as you add it. When dough is wet enough to come together and form a ball, gently knead the dough a few times, not too much.

Separate into 1½-inch balls.

Gently (carefully) place the dumplings into the stockpot, on top of the chicken meat. Some will fall into the broth, that is okay.

Gently boil 10 minutes with no lid on.

Gently boil 10 more minutes with the lid on.

Make the Gravy

Melt butter in large skillet on medium-high heat.

When butter has melted, whisk in flour quickly until it is more of a paste and all of it has been mixed well into the butter.

Carefully add milk and seasonings, and whisk until it is well blended.

Slowly add in chicken broth a little at a time, whisking the whole time.

Continue to add chicken broth until you get a nice saucy gravy. Once the dumplings are finished cooking, pour the gravy into stock pot and mix well, careful not to tear apart the dumplings too much as you mix.

Serve hot with homemade bread and a side salad or vegetable dish.

ANNIE'S WHITE CHILI WITH CHICKEN

Ingredients

3 T. olive oil

2 cups diced onion

3 cups chopped, boneless skinless chicken breast (bite-size pieces)

1 T. finely minced garlic

1 quart chicken stock

3 (15 oz.) cans northern beans, drained and rinsed

1 cup frozen corn or canned corn

2 (4.5 oz.) cans diced green chiles

1 T. dried oregano leaves

2 tsp. ground cumin

2 tsp. ground coriander

Directions

Heat olive oil in a 4-quart pot or large skillet over medium heat.

Add onion, and sauté until soft.

Add chicken, and sauté until no longer pink.

Stir in garlic, and sauté about 30 seconds.

Add chicken stock, beans, corn, chiles, oregano, cumin, and coriander.

Turn heat to low and simmer 20 minutes.

Serve in bowls garnished with shredded cheese, sour cream and/or crushed tortilla chips.

"SUPPER'S READY!" CHICKEN CASSEROLE

Ingredients

3 (12.5 oz.) cans chicken breast, drained (or use 4 ½ cups pre-cooked and diced fresh chicken)

2 cups (16 oz.) sour cream

1 (10.5 oz.) can cream of mushroom soup

1 (10.5 oz.) can cream of chicken soup

2 cups chicken broth

½ cup chopped celery

1 onion

2 T. butter

4 cups herb-seasoned stuffing

Directions

Preheat oven to 350°. Combine chicken, sour cream, and soups in a large bowl. Stir until thoroughly mixed.

Pour chicken mixture into a 9 x 13-inch casserole dish.

In a 2-quart saucepan, heat broth, celery, and onion over medium heat to a boil then reduce heat to low, cover, and cook 5 minutes until vegetables are tender.

Add butter to broth.

Add stuffing to broth and mix lightly.

Evenly distribute stuffing on top of chicken mixture.

Bake for approximately 20 minutes or until stuffing is brown and chicken mixture is bubbly.

Serve with your favorite cranberry sauce.

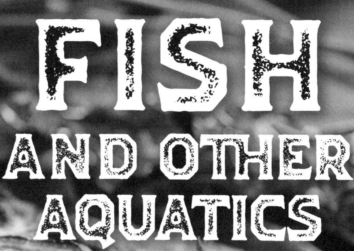

Part Four

FISH
AND OTHER
AQUATICS

Fish

JUST ADD WATER

As a dad who immensely enjoys fishing, when our children were very young I (Steve) took them with me and learned an important lesson: If you want to be with your kids, take them fishing. *If you want to fish, don't take your kids.*

Trying to do serious fishing with kids around is almost impossible. Really, it's even downright dangerous. I struggled a bit with this reality, but thankfully I came to realize that having Heidi and Nathan with me was the point—not the fishing. For that reason, I didn't really mind that we'd get tangled up in the line or that I risked getting a hook embedded in my jaw or backside as a result of a cast gone astray.

Because I was determined to prioritize our togetherness over merely catching fish, I now have great memories to recall. And because I had ample opportunities to practice what I preach, I feel qualified to write this song for dads who have young kids and an appreciation for angling. It's actually a recipe for some real fun!

JUST ADD WATER

If you want to make a sweet memory
　with your kids
Here's the recipe
Peanut butter and a jar of jam
Loaf of bread and pop in a can
Bamboo poles and hooks on the line
Can of worms and some of your time
And don't forget that little round bobber
Then all you do is just add water

Just add water, don't have to be deep
Take 'em to the banks of a big lake or
　a little creek
Sweet memories with your sons and
　your daughters
That's what you'll get when you just
　add water

You can take your phone, but leave it off
Turn on your heart, and let it talk
'Cause words come easy when you're fishing
And when they talk, make sure you listen
If the weather turns hot and the fish go hide
Don't pack it up and run back inside
Just tell the kids, "Do like your father!"
Roll up your pants and just add water

Just add water, don't have to be deep
Take 'em to the banks of a big lake or
　a little creek
Sweet memories with your sons and
　your daughters
That's what you'll get when you just
　add water

Red Snapper

RED SNAPPER JUBILEE

Ingredients

2 red snapper fillets

Butter-flavored cooking spray

4 T. butter

1 medium garlic clove, minced

3 to 4 drops Worcestershire sauce

½ tsp. Creole seasoning

⅛ tsp. ground black pepper

1 tsp. minced fresh parsley

1 tsp. chopped fresh chive

4 T. seasoned breadcrumbs

2 T. grated Parmesan cheese

When our kids were younger, one of our choices for a fishing spot took us to a place where the water was much deeper than the creeks or lakes near our house. Heidi, Nathan, and I (Steve) fished in the Gulf of Mexico out of Gulfport, Mississippi. The red snapper were plentiful! After two days of arm-tiring tugging to bring in our catch, Annie used some great recipes to turn our hard work into a feast. This is one of her favorites.

Directions

Preheat oven to 400° and use the cooking spray to grease a medium-size baking dish. Put red snapper fillets in the baking dish.

Melt butter in a cast-iron skillet. Add garlic, Worcestershire sauce, Creole seasoning, pepper, parsley, and chive. Cook at low heat for about 2 minutes.

Brush both sides of the fillets with the herb and butter combination. Sprinkle the fillets with the breadcrumbs and Parmesan cheese.

Bake for 10 to 12 minutes (thickness of fillets determines baking time). When the fish flakes and is no longer translucent, it is done.

Tip: Serve with Chapman's Chin-Lickin'-Good Hush Puppies (page 167) and Coleslaw (page 148).

 TIPS ON COOKING FISH

- Fish with scales need to have the scales removed. "Scaling" is easier if vinegar is rubbed on the fish first.

- Rub oil on fish before grilling to keep the meat from becoming too dry.

PERFECT PAN-SEARED RED SNAPPER

Ingredients

2 (4 oz.) fillets red snapper

1 T. olive oil

1 lemon, juiced

2 T. rice wine vinegar

1 T. honey

1 tsp. Dijon mustard

¼ cup chopped green onions

1 tsp. dried ground ginger

Directions

Using cold water, rinse the snapper and pat dry with paper towels.

In a shallow bowl, mix the rest of the ingredients.

Heat a well-seasoned cast-iron skillet on the stove using medium temperature. Dip snapper fillets in liquid mixture, coating both sides. Place in skillet and cook 2 to 3 minutes per side.

Pour remaining marinade into skillet. Lower heat and simmer for 2 to 3 minutes. When fish flakes easily with a fork, it is ready to serve.

Cobia

HEIDI HOLDS THE RECORD

When Nathan, Heidi, and I (Steve) left the Gulfport, Mississippi, dock in the big charter boat, we didn't know the two-day excursion would end with the boys being totally out-fished by the only girl in the group. The cobia (Lemon fish) were running in the Gulf of Mexico, and we'd like to say "We wore 'em out," but the truth is they wore us out.

Nathan yanked for quite a while on a 42-pounder before landing it. I got into a nice 29-pound brute, fighting it for at least twenty minutes. We thought we were kings of the boat until Heidi hooked the big one. She sat strapped into a chair hanging on tight to what turned out to be a 54-pound cobia. She wrestled that monster for a good forty minutes. I helped some, Nathan helped a little, but Heidi was the one who landed that whale of a fish. She deserves full credit! To this day she holds the record on the Chapman Family Wall of Fin Fame.

GRILLED COBIA WITH LEMON PEPPER

Ingredients

1 cobia fillet, skinned

Olive oil

Lemon pepper

Garlic powder

Fresh dill

Lemon juice

Directions

Lightly rub cobia fillet with olive oil. Season with lemon pepper and garlic powder.

Start a charcoal grill, letting temperature rise very hot. Place fillet on grill, but not directly over the heat source. Cook for 6 to 7 minutes. Turn fillet and grill another 6 to 7 minutes, still over indirect heat.

Remove the cobia from the grill and allow it to rest, letting the juices settle. Sprinkle with fresh dill and lemon juice.

Tip: Serve with Homemade Tartar Sauce (page 195).

 Salmon

HEIDI'S WONDERFUL SALMON

Ingredients

2 cloves garlic, minced

½ cup light olive oil

1 tsp. dried basil

1 tsp. kosher salt

1 tsp. ground black pepper

1 T. lemon juice (fresh or concentrate)

1 T. chopped fresh parsley

2 large salmon fillets

My all-time favorite fish to eat is salmon, and my (Steve) favorite way to eat it is how my daughter, Heidi, makes it. There's something about the taste of wild salmon that tempts me to run everybody off so I can hoard all the fillets. Thankfully, Heidi usually makes more than enough to feed everyone—and often sends me home with leftovers!

Directions

Preheat oven to 375°.

In a medium glass bowl, combine the garlic, olive oil, basil, salt, pepper, lemon juice, and parsley. Mix thoroughly.

Place salmon fillets in a separate glass bowl. Pour the liquid over the fillets, and marinate in the refrigerator for an hour, turning occasionally.

Remove salmon from marinade. Place the fillets in enough aluminum foil that the edges curl up to hold in liquid. Pour in all the marinade and crimp the edges of the foil to seal. Place the foil-covered salmon in a glass dish.

Bake for 35 to 45 minutes. You'll know the salmon is ready when the flesh easily flakes with a fork.

Tip: Serve with baked potato and Asparagus Tomato Supreme (page 148).

SALMON CAKES

Ingredients

1 (14.7 oz.) can pink salmon

1 egg

1 onion, finely chopped

½ cup milk

1 cup flour

¼ cup cooking oil

Directions

Empty the salmon into a small bowl. Add the egg, milk, and onion. Stir well.

Form into biscuit-size cakes and roll in flour.

Fry in hot oil until golden brown.

Serve with tartar sauce (page 195), ketchup, or cocktail sauce (page 195).

Trout

LEMONY TROUT ALMONDINE

Ingredients

4 lbs. trout

Salt and pepper

¾ cup flour

2 T. olive oil

2 T. butter, divided

¾ cup slivered almonds

1 T. lemon juice

Directions

Season trout with salt and pepper. Dredge trout in flour.

In a skillet, heated to medium high, add oil and 1 tablespoon of butter. Add fish and cook 3 to 4 minutes on each side until light brown.

Remove fish from the pan, cover, and keep warm.

Using the same pan, add 1 tablespoon of butter, heating to medium high. When the butter is melted, add the almonds and sauté. Add the lemon juice and heat through.

Place the trout on a serving plate. Spoon almond mixture over the fish and serve.

EASY TROUT

Ingredients

2 trout fillets

1 cup milk

¾ cup flour

1 tsp. salt

½ tsp. pepper

1 stick butter

Directions

In a bowl, soak the trout fillets in milk for 5 minutes.

Combine flour, salt, and pepper in a shallow pan, and dip the trout into the mixture to coat both sides.

Melt butter on medium heat. Fry trout until golden brown and the flesh of the fish flakes. Cook each side 3 to 4 minutes.

Catfish

THOSE CREEPY CATFISH...MMMM!

O f all the fish my (Annie) dad brought home, my least favorite to see were the buckets of live, just-caught catfish. I guess it was the whiskers and the mean glint in their eyes that gave me pause. I gladly stood aside to let my brothers kill and clean the slimy things.

But when the cleaning work ended and the cooking started, my opinion of the creepy fish changed dramatically. Here are the recipes our family so enjoyed. They helped me get past the disconcerting expressions of the beady-eyed swimmers. I hope you enjoy them too!

CATFISH STEW

Ingredients

2 (10 oz.) cans tomato soup

2 (10 oz.) cans water

1 (16 oz.) bottle ketchup

4 T. Worcestershire sauce

2 tsp. salt

1 T. black pepper

1 T. hot sauce

½ lb. bacon or salt pork

3 large onions, chopped

4 or 5 lbs. catfish (chunked or filleted)

Directions

Place the first 7 ingredients in a large pot and cook over low heat.

Dice the bacon and fry over medium heat. Remove bacon and sauté onion in the bacon grease until tender. Add to soup mixture.

Simmer for 30 minutes.

If desired, lightly salt the catfish. Add to soup mixture.

Simmer 12 to 15 minutes. When done, the fish should flake when tested with a fork.

Tip: Serve over steamed rice.

GRILLED CATFISH

Ingredients

2 lbs. catfish

Basting Sauce

1 stick butter, melted

⅔ cup lemon juice

Dash of hot sauce

1 tsp. mustard

2 T. Worcestershire sauce

1 tsp. salt

1 tsp. ground pepper

1 tsp. chili powder

Directions

Wash the catfish meat in cold water and pat dry.

Whisk together basting sauce ingredients.

Place catfish on a well-oiled grill or grilling basket over medium heat or coals for approximately 20 minutes. While grilling, baste the catfish frequently with the sauce. Turn fish over and grill for another 15 minutes, continuing to baste often. When fish flakes easily with a fork, it's ready.

PECAN-COATED FRIED CATFISH

Ingredients

1 cup pecan pieces

1 cup buttermilk

2 eggs

1 tsp. hot sauce

½ cup flour

1 cup cornmeal

1 tsp. salt

1 tsp. pepper

2 to 2½ lbs. catfish

Nonstick cooking oil

Directions

Preheat oven to 350°. Toast the pecans by placing them in a dry skillet over medium heat. Stir constantly until pecans are golden brown. (Be careful because they burn easily and quickly.) Place the toasted nuts in a food processor and grind until the consistency of meal. Set aside.

In a shallow bowl, stir together buttermilk, eggs, and hot sauce.

In a separate dish, stir together flour, cornmeal, pecans, salt, and pepper.

Wash the catfish in cold water and pat dry. Dip the fillets into the buttermilk mixture and then into the cornmeal mixture. After coating each fillet well, set it aside on a piece of waxed paper until ready to cook.

Place fillets on a greased pan.

Bake for 20 minutes or until meat is brown and flakes easily with a fork.

Tip: Serve with Chapman's Chin-Lickin'-Good Hush Puppies (page 167) and Coleslaw (page 148).

Walleye

DEEP-FRIED WALLEYE

Ingredients

8 oz. (2 sleeves) saltine crackers

1 tsp. garlic powder

1 tsp. pepper

2 to 3 lbs. fresh walleye fillets, skinned (or yellow perch)

2 eggs

1 cup milk

Corn or canola oil, 1-inch deep in skillet

Directions

Using a blender, grind the saltine crackers to almost flour consistency. Add garlic powder and pepper and mix well. Put in a shallow bowl or plate.

Cut fish into pieces and set aside.

In a large bowl, whip eggs with milk.

Dip pieces of fish in milk mixture, and then dredge in cracker flour, coating the fish well. Place fish on a paper towel-covered plate.

In a deep skillet, heat cooking oil to 400°. Carefully drop fish pieces into the hot oil.

Deep-fry fish 3 minutes per side (pieces will float when done). Remove fish from oil and place on several layers of paper towels to drain. Pat dry and serve.

BROILED FISH PARMESAN

Ingredients

¼ cup milk (or buttermilk)

1 lb. fish

2 T. Parmesan cheese

½ cup breadcrumbs

½ tsp. paprika

1 tsp. salt

½ tsp. pepper

1 tsp. garlic salt

Nonstick cooking spray

1 T. butter, melted

Directions

Pour milk into a medium-size mixing bowl. Place the fillets in the bowl, coating each piece.

In a separate bowl, combine dry ingredients.

Dredge the milk-covered fillets in the dry mixture, coating each piece well.

Place the fillets on a baking dish sprayed with oil. Dribble melted butter on each piece of fish.

Broil at 425° for 15 minutes or until golden brown.

Bass

BATTERED BASS

Ingredients

2 cups flour

1 cup cornmeal

1 tsp. salt

1 tsp. pepper

6 to 8 bass fillets, boned

1 cup milk

½ cup vegetable oil

Directions

Combine all dry ingredients in a large ziplock bag.

Pour the milk into a shallow bowl. Soak the fillets in milk for 1 to 2 minutes.

Removing one fillet at a time, place it in the plastic bag with the seasonings and shake, coating thoroughly.

Pour the vegetable oil into a heavy skillet and heat on medium-high. Put fillets in skillet, being careful not to crowd them. Fry until golden brown, approximately 4 minutes on each side. Remove from skillet and drain on paper towels.

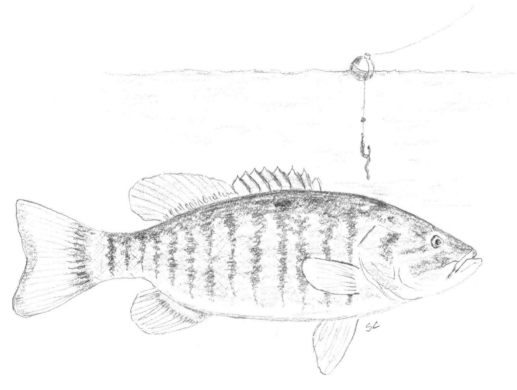

Bluegill

LILY'S FIRST FISH

On a late afternoon, our daughter, Heidi, and her husband, Emmitt, along with their two daughters, were visiting our home. Evening dinner was three or four hours away, so I (Steve) suggested we use the time to head out to the big lake at Coldstream Christian Camp near Adams, Tennessee, for a quick wetting of fishing line. Our oldest granddaughter, Lily, jumped on the idea like it was a trampoline. (I'd bought three tubs of night crawlers at a local convenience store, fully expecting her thrilled reaction to the idea of going fishing.)

Within 45 minutes, Lily, Emmitt, and I were pushing off into the calm lake in one canoe, while Heidi was pushing off in another. Five minutes later we were fishing. I did the paddling and positioning near the known "hot spots," while Emmitt took care of the dangerous job of baiting Lily's hook as she held the rod and reel. He knew that one mischievous jerk of the pole by his loving daughter and he might be digging a barbed hook out of his hand. Fortunately for him, Lily was compliant with the policy of not moving when her daddy was pinching a hook between his fingers.

I was thrilled to be within two feet of my precious grand-girl when the bobber on her line disappeared and she felt the tug through the pole for the very first time. It doesn't get any better than that!

Emmitt quickly encouraged, "Set the hook, Lily!" He'd schooled her on how to do it, and she was a quick study. Without hesitating, she sharply lifted the tip of her rod into the air. Suddenly the tip of the pole was dancing. Her eyes widened as she squealed with excitement. She cranked the reel handle, and within a few seconds she hoisted a bluegill out of the water. Her prize was a little bigger than her hand—a perfect first catch.

Emmitt reached for the line to steady his daughter's finned trophy, and that's when Lily turned to make sure her Papa—me!—was watching. I was indeed. The following recipe is a tasty way to honor any kid's first catch. (Bear in mind that it takes several bluegill to make enough for a meal.)

BATTER-FRIED BLUEGILL

Ingredients	Directions
Ice-cold water	Prepare the batter by mixing ice-cold water with the fry mix. (Ice-cold water helps the batter stick to the fillets.)
2 cups fry coating mix	
3 cups peanut oil	Pour oil into a skillet and heat to 350° on medium-high. Coat the fish with the batter evenly.
1 lb. bluegill, filleted and boned	
Salt	Place coated fish in the skillet and cook until golden brown, 2 to 3 minutes per side.
	Remove fish from oil and drain on paper towels. Season with salt and serve.

Frog Legs

JUMPIN' FROG LEGS

Ingredients

3 T. cooking oil

6 to 8 frog legs

½ cup all-purpose flour

Salt and pepper

Directions

In a large iron skillet, heat oil to medium hot.

Coat the frog legs with flour.

Put the frog legs in a single layer in the skillet. Fry slowly, turning once. (If needed, add a little more oil.) Season with salt and pepper after turning.

Cook for 15 minutes or until golden brown. (Do not over-cook. You don't want the meat to fall off the bones.) Serve hot.

Tip: Keep the skillet lid handy. Sometimes as the legs heat, they jump as if trying to get out of the skillet!

FRIED FROG LEGS

Ingredients

2 eggs, beaten

2 T. mayonnaise

1 T. cornstarch

1 T. lemon juice

½ tsp. baking soda

1 tsp. salt

½ tsp. pepper

2 lbs. frog legs

2 cups canola oil

⅔ cup all-purpose flour

⅓ cup Italian breadcrumbs

Directions

To make a marinade, combine the eggs, mayo, cornstarch, lemon juice, baking soda, salt, and pepper. Pour into a large ziplock bag.

Place frog legs in the marinade and seal. Refrigerate for 24 hours, turning the bag a couple of times to fully marinate the meat.

In a heavy skillet, pour in canola oil to 1-inch depth and heat to 350°.

Mix the flour and breadcrumbs in a ziplock bag.

Remove the frog legs from the marinade, allowing the liquid to drain off. Dredge the legs in the flour/breadcrumb mixture.

Fry the legs in the hot oil until golden brown, approximately 5 minutes per side, turning only once.

Tip: Serve with Becky's Potato Soup (page 156).

Turtle

WRESTLING RIVER FARM TURTLES

In my (Annie) opinion, turtle falls into the category of foods that I call "Who in the world looked at that and said, 'I'm gonna kill that thing and eat it!'" I suppose the answer to that categorical question would be "Somebody who was really hungry." Obviously, turtle is not a first-choice dish for me. Still, there are many who don't require being near starvation to enjoy a serving of it. My dad was among those brave eaters. He not only loved to consume turtle, he liked finding them and bringing them home. My sister, Alice, six years my senior, shared with me some tense-filled memories of turtle hunting with Dad:

> As a 12-year-old girl, I recall going with my father to the back waters of the Kanawha River to capture a turtle so Mother could make one of Dad's favorite meals—turtle soup.
>
> It was along the tree-lined banks that the turtles preferred to hide. What a thrill to see a head bob up from time to time. Dad had figured out that he could tell the direction they were perched on the tree roots that were submerged under the murky waters by the way their heads rose above the surface.
>
> On this particular trip, after spotting a turtle about the size of the average automobile hubcap, my dad was about to take off his shoes and go into the creek. I, never fearing much of anything (including the snakes that called the creek home), announced I wanted to capture the shelled beast. Not hesitating, I proceeded to wade over to the turtle. As I pressed through the muddy bed of the creek in waist-high water, Dad cautioned that when I grabbed the turtle I should place my hands right on it, one on each side of the shell at its midsection.
>
> Once I reached the turtle, I knew there was no turning back. When I grabbed the thing by the shell, the hind legs violently thrashed. Being up close and personal to the sight of its sharp toenails, no one had to tell me that it was going to hurt really badly if they connected with my skin. I thought for a brief moment about tossing the heavy turtle out into the creek, but when I got a glimpse of the proud look on Dad's face, I was determined to hold on.
>
> With the turtle's legs still swinging wildly, I wheeled around in the mud that sucked at my feet. I headed as fast as I could toward the bank. It felt like I was running through cold molasses. And holding the unhappy turtle at shoulder level was not easy either. After what seemed a full minute to make the short run to solid ground, I'll never forget the feeling of satisfaction when Dad smiled at my brave accomplishment. His joy was even greater when Mother transformed the ugly water crawler into one of Dad's favorite dishes that evening. We still refer to it as "N.R.'s River Farm Turtle Stew."

N.R.'S RIVER FARM TURTLE STEW

Ingredients

3 lbs. turtle meat

3 T. butter

3 T. flour

1 lb. onions, chopped

2 cloves garlic, chopped

1 (4 oz.) can tomato paste

3 T. canola oil

2 (15 oz.) cans tomatoes

¼ cup chopped celery

1 cup chopped green onions

1 cup chopped bell pepper

⅛ tsp. cayenne pepper

4 bay leaves

8 whole cloves

½ tsp. allspice

1 T. sugar

3 T. cider vinegar

Directions

Parboil turtle meat (put meat in a pot, add water to completely cover it, and boil for 10 minutes). Drain off water and let cool. Cut into pieces and set aside.

Make a roux: Combine butter and flour. Add onion, garlic, and tomato paste. Cook on low heat for 20 minutes.

Add the turtle meat to the roux, along with enough water to cover the meat. Cook until the liquid is reduced by half.

Add the remaining ingredients, stir, and cook for 30 minutes. Check to see if it needs more water to keep meat covered. Simmer for 3 hours.

Tip: Serve with Sylvie Biscuits (page 163).

Part Five

"SERVE WITH" SUGGESTIONS

Vegetables and Salads
A HOME GARDEN—WANTED OR NEEDED

My (Annie) mother and dad returned to their farm after their one-day honeymoon prepared to tend to their only source of livelihood—a herd of hogs. But what they discovered was heartbreaking. A neighbor had some hogs that had died with cholera and instead of burying the carcasses he threw them in an open ditch. Dogs had found the dead hogs and dragged some remains onto my parent's property and infected their herd. They saw that some of the hogs were already showing signs of sickness and they knew their only choice was to kill and bury their financial future. As they worked together that day my mother tearfully said to her young groom, "I'll raise a garden from now on and we'll never be hungry like this again."

This story makes the point that while some folks *want* to grow a garden, others *need* to do it. Perhaps you simply want the enjoyment and satisfaction of raising your own food, or maybe you now have a "need to" reason for growing a garden, such as eating healthier. If so, you may need some instruction on how to get started.

MAMA'S FRESH-FROM-THE-GARDEN GREEN BEANS

Ingredients

2 lbs. fresh green beans

Butter, bacon grease, or olive oil

Sugar (optional)

Salt

Minced garlic (optional)

When I (Annie) was a kid, if I was found weeding Mom's garden it was likely because I had used a five-letter word that she considered forbidden. The word was "bored." There's a good chance I cut down more plants than weeds, but there was no way to get out of the sentence handed down for my unacceptable language. I didn't like the process, but I sure enjoyed the product of what I reluctantly helped grow.

One of the veggies I labored for and especially enjoyed was the snap green beans. We'd gather them in a bushel basket and sit on the porch, snap the beans, and talk. Now, when I taste green beans, either fresh or canned, my mind goes back to those days. Here's one of Mom's favorite recipes.

Directions

Trim each end of the bean and snap it in thirds. Wash beans in cold water then put in a large heavy pot and cover with water. Bring to boil.

Reduce heat to medium and simmer until beans are tender.

Drain the water and place the beans in a large, nonstick skillet.

Melt butter or use bacon grease or olive oil (amount determined by size of skillet) in the skillet and toss with the beans. If desired, add small amount of granulated sugar. Salt to taste, and add optional garlic at this point.

Slowly simmer the beans until moisture evaporates and beans are caramelized (be careful not to burn the beans).

HALF RUNNER GREEN BEANS

Ingredients

3 lbs. half runner green beans, fresh

3 beef bouillon cubes

2 T. bacon drippings (or vegetable oil)

¾ cup water

Directions

String and wash beans. Put green beans in a 6-quart pressure cooker. Add the beef cubes, bacon drippings, and water.

Put the lid on the pressure cooker and set for 15 pounds pressure. When the pressure gauge starts making noise, reduce heat and cook for 15 minutes.

Tip: Reduce the pressure in the pan by running cold water over the cooker in the sink to speed up the cooling process.

ASPARAGUS TOMATO SUPREME

Ingredients

Asparagus

Cherry tomatoes

Olive oil

Salt

Pepper

Directions

Preheat oven to 350°. Trim off the woody stems of the asparagus. Wash the tender asparagus and then spread out on a large cookie sheet.

Place cherry tomatoes among the asparagus. Drizzle with olive oil and season with salt and pepper.

Bake until the asparagus is limp and the tomatoes are plumped up, approximately 20 minutes.

QUICK AND EASY SALSA

Ingredients

1 (28 oz.) can diced tomatoes

1 (10 oz.) can Rotel tomatoes

1 onion, diced

1 bunch of cilantro, chopped

1 green pepper

Directions

In a food processor add all the ingredients and mix. Refrigerate and serve.

COLESLAW

Ingredients

1 head cabbage

1 carrot

1 green pepper

Salt and pepper to taste

Marzetti's Cole Slaw Dressing*

Directions

Shred or grate a head of cabbage into a bowl. Grate the carrot and green pepper into the bowl. Add salt and pepper to taste.

Add dressing until you get the consistency and taste you desire.

* You can also make your own dressing: 1 cup mayonnaise, 2 T. sugar, and 2 T. apple cider vinegar.

BROCCOLI AND CAULIFLOWER COLESLAW

Ingredients

1 (8 oz.) pkg. shredded broccoli and cauliflower

½ cup cranberries

⅛ cup sunflower or pumpkin seeds

½ cup golden raisins

1 small red delicious apple, chopped

½ cup coleslaw dressing

Directions

Mix all ingredients and chill.

Tip: This is a nice variation on traditional coleslaw. Even though my family loves the simple shredded cabbage and mayonnaise coleslaw, they have come to appreciate the mixture of flavors in this twist on coleslaw. The green of the broccoli and the texture of the cauliflower adds visual and taste appeal.

QUICK COLESLAW SALAD

Ingredients

1 (8 oz.) pkg. shredded cabbage

1 carrot, shredded

¼ cup cranberries

¼ cup sunflower or pumpkin seeds

¼ cup golden raisins

1 small red delicious apple, chopped

Coleslaw dressing, to taste

Directions

Mix all ingredients and chill before serving.

GREEN AND WHITE SALAD

Ingredients

1 head cauliflower, chopped into small pieces

1 head broccoli, chopped fine

1 (16 oz.) pkg. frozen peas

8 slices bacon, fried and chopped into small pieces

¾ cup Miracle Whip or mayonnaise

1 cup sour cream

1 tsp. salt

1 tsp. sugar

4 to 6 green onions, chopped fine

Dash of garlic powder

Directions

Mix all ingredients together the day prior to serving. This salad keeps well in the refrigerator.

TEN STEPS TO STARTING AN URBAN FOOD GARDEN

BY JAN LEARY

The lack of acreage or farmland is no reason for you to delay growing some of your own food. It's easy and fun! Here are ten steps needed to get started and join the family of happy gardeners.

1. Choose the sunniest part of your backyard, patio, or balcony. This is where you're going to put a couple of containers to start. Full sun means at least six hours of sunlight.
2. Make sure you grow what you like to eat. The easiest summer vegetables for beginners are lettuce, cucumbers, summer squash, and tomatoes. You can grow from seed or purchase plant starts. I suggest purchasing plant starts if this is your first effort.
3. Choose your container and make sure it has drainage holes in the bottom (or drill a few holes in the bottom of a plastic or wood container). If you use fabric grow bags, you won't need to worry about drainage holes.
4. Next, purchase potting soil (mix). Avoid garden soil because it's too heavy for containers. Plus, as a beginner, you'll like the fact that most potting mix comes with fertilizer already in it.
5. Buy or borrow a trowel (hand shovel) for digging. If you want to be extra cute or clean, buy gardening gloves.
6. Once you have all the components: a sunny space, seeds or plant starts, a container and potting mix, then you are ready to grow. Gather everything and get ready to start your garden.
7. Fill your container with potting mix about two-thirds full, then water the soil well. Tap the pot on the ground a few times to get out any air bubbles.
8. Place your plant into the center of the container with one hand and with the other fill the remainder of the pot with potting mix until an inch or so from the top. Water the plant well, press around the roots so there is good soil-to-root contact.
9. Once the plant is in place, cover the remaining inch at the top of the container with a natural mulch, i.e., dried leaves, natural wood chips, etc.
10. Watch your plant and wait for the food to show up. Press your finger into the soil about an inch every couple of days. If it feels dry, then add a little water.

BROCCOLI CAULIFLOWER SALAD

Ingredients

Dressing

½ cup light mayonnaise

¼ cup sugar

1 T. vinegar

1 T. minced garlic

Salad

1 large head broccoli, chopped

1 small head cauliflower, chopped

8 slices bacon, fried crispy

4 oz. shredded Swiss cheese

Directions

Mix the first four ingredients to make the dressing.

In a separate bowl, combine the broccoli, cauliflower, crumbled bacon, and cheese.

Add dressing, toss, and chill before serving.

This salad can be made the night before so all the flavors have time to mingle.

You can also adjust how much dressing you use so you get the flavor without drowning the broccoli and cauliflower. This will save a few calories so you can have dessert!

CORN CASSEROLE

Ingredients

4 large eggs

⅔ cup safflower oil

1 tsp. garlic salt

1 (8.5 oz.) box corn muffin mix

2 (14.75 oz.) cans cream-style corn

Nonstick cooking spray

½ cup grated cheddar cheese

This is a family favorite that seems to show up and show off nearly every time we get together.

Directions

Preheat oven to 375°.

Crack eggs into a large bowl and beat well. Add oil and garlic salt, mixing well. Stir in the dry muffin mix and cream corn until well blended.

Pour into greased baking pan, and sprinkle grated cheese on top.

Bake for 50 to 60 minutes or until brown, puffed on top, and the sides are slightly pulled away from the pan.

Remove from oven and let set 5 to 10 minutes.

Tip: Great served hot or at room temperature.

THREE CORN CASSEROLE

Ingredients

1 (15.25 oz.) can whole kernel corn, drained

1 (14.75 oz.) can cream-style corn

1 (8.5 oz.) box cornbread mix

1 stick of butter

1 (8 oz.) container sour cream

Nonstick cooking spray

Directions

Preheat oven to 350°. Mix all ingredients and place in casserole dish sprayed with nonstick cooking spray. Bake for 1 hour.

QUICK AND EASY MICROWAVE CORN ON THE COB

Ingredients

Corn on the cob

Butter and salt to taste

With our kids raised, it's usually just the two of us sharing a meal. Sometimes we get a hankering for fresh grown corn on the cob. Here are a couple of ways to cook just one or two ears. (This helps if you're carb conscious.)

Directions

Option 1

Shuck an ear of corn, removing husks and silk.

Rinse in cold water. Wrap a wet paper towel around the ear (of corn, that is). Place in microwave on high setting for 4 minutes.

Be careful removing the corn. It will be very hot.

Butter and salt to taste, and thank us later!

Option 2

Select an ear of corn. Check to make sure there are no worms inside the husk (peel the husk back an inch or two and you'll know).

With a sharp kitchen knife cut top and bottom off the ear.

Place ear in the microwave on high setting for 4 minutes.

Be careful removing the corn since it will be very hot.

Remove the husk and silk.

Butter and salt to taste—and keep a napkin handy for your chin!

YUMMY BUTTERY STOVETOP CORN ON THE COB

Ingredients

3 ears corn, shucked, washed, and halved

6 cups water

1 cup milk

½ stick butter

1 tsp. salt

Directions

Combine water, milk, butter, and salt in a cooking pot deep enough to avoid boil over.

Bring water and ingredients to a boil. Add corn and reduce heat to a medium simmer.

Cook for 10 minutes and then turn off heat, leaving the corn in the pot until ready to serve.

MASHED POTATOES

Ingredients

8 medium potatoes, washed and peeled

½ tsp. salt

4 T. butter

¼ cup milk

½ cup sour cream

Directions

Cut potatoes into small chunks. Put into a 2-quart pan, add salt, and bring to boil. Cover and cook slowly until potatoes are tender, 15 to 20 minutes.

Strain out the water, add the butter, and cover until butter melts.

Use a hand mixer to mash the potatoes in the pan they were cooked in. Add milk and sour cream and beat until creamy. Add more milk and butter until you get the texture you desire. Serve hot.

FIREPLACE BAKED POTATOES

Ingredients

Baking potatoes

Salt

Butter

Directions

Use as many potatoes as you want, and you don't need to wash them. Bury the potatoes in the coals and let them cook for 15 to 20 minutes. If desired, you can wrap them in foil.

Pull them out of the coals and poke with a fork to see if they're done (fork should enter potatoes easily). If done, carefully wipe the skins clean.

Cut potatoes in half, add salt and butter, and serve hot.

EVELYN'S POTATO SALAD

Ingredients

10 medium russet potatoes

¼ cup grated Parmesan cheese

8 hard-boiled eggs, chopped

1 medium carrot, grated

4 medium radishes, grated

½ small onion, chopped

3 T. green olives, sliced with pimentos

1 (8 oz.) jar sweet pickles, chopped

½ head of cauliflower, cut into small
   pieces

2 tsp. celery seeds

2 cups mayonnaise

Directions

Place unpeeled potatoes in a large kettle and cover with water. Bring to boil, reduce heat, and boil gently until potatoes are tender, 15 to 20 minutes.

Drain the water, let the potatoes cool, and then peel and cube them.

Place the potatoes in a large bowl and sprinkle with Parmesan cheese. Gently stir. Add all other ingredients except for the mayonnaise and mix gently.

Place mayonnaise in a medium bowl. Beat with a spoon to make it easier to stir into the salad. Add the mayo to the potato mixture a little bit at a time until you get the consistency and taste you desire.

Serve immediately or refrigerate overnight.

MOUNTAINEER CRISPY POTATO WEDGES

Ingredients

2 russet potatoes, scrubbed and
   cut into eighths

½ tsp. salt

½ cup olive oil

1 T. garlic powder

1 tsp. smoked paprika

1 tsp. onion powder

1 tsp. chopped rosemary leaves

1 tsp. thyme leaves

½ tsp. black pepper

Directions

Preheat oven to 400° (or use air fryer).

Place potato wedges in a cooking pot and cover with water. Bring to boil then simmer 10 minutes or until medium soft.

Gently pour cooked potatoes in colander and drain.

In a bowl combine all spices and olive oil and stir together.

Add potatoes and gently toss with spice and oil mixture.

Spread wedges evenly on a cookie sheet lined with foil.

Place in oven and bake until crispy brown.

Receive accolades graciously!

SWEET, SWEET POTATO CASSEROLE

Ingredients

3 cups sweet potatoes, freshly cooked or canned, and mashed

1 cup white sugar

1 tsp. vanilla

½ cup melted butter

2 eggs, beaten

Nonstick cooking spray

Topping

1 cup light brown sugar

⅓ cup all-purpose flour

½ cup chopped pecans

¼ cup butter, not melted

Directions

Preheat oven to 350°. Mix all ingredients together and put in a greased casserole dish.

Mix topping ingredients until crumbly, and sprinkle over sweet potato mixture.

Bake for 30 minutes.

GREAT AND EASY BAKED BEANS

Ingredients

2 lbs. dry white Great Northern beans

1 (40 oz.) bottle ketchup

1 cup brown sugar

2 tsp. yellow mustard

1 small onion, chopped

10 slices bacon, fried and crumbled

2 T. bacon grease

Dried red pepper flakes

Directions

Wash the beans and remove any rocks and grit. Put them in a large kettle and cover with water. Bring to boil for 5 minutes. Pour off water, and refill with clean water. Bring to boil again.

Lower the heat and cook slowly until beans are almost done, but not soft. If needed, add additional water to cover the beans.

Put in most of the ketchup and brown sugar, and all the mustard, onion, bacon, bacon grease, and red pepper flakes.

Stir well and taste. If desired, add more ketchup and brown sugar. Add water if mixture is too dry to pour.

Pour the bean mixture into a 9 x 12 x 2-inch roaster or baking dish. Cover tightly with foil.

Bake at 350° for 1 hour. Remove the foil and bake for another 40 minutes or until beans are tender.

Tip: These baked beans are good served hot or cold.

BECKY'S POTATO SOUP

Ingredients

48 oz. chicken broth, divided

6 potatoes, peeled and cubed

½ tsp. Mrs. Dash Original Seasoning

1 stick butter

2 (12 oz.) pkgs. frozen chopped onions
   (or 4 cups diced onion)

½ cup all-purpose flour

1¼ cups instant potatoes

1 qt. half-and-half

Salt and pepper

Cheddar cheese, grated (optional)

Bacon bits (optional)

Directions

Pour chicken broth into a large pot. Add potatoes and Mrs. Dash Original Seasoning. Cook at a quiet boil for 15 to 20 minutes, until potatoes are tender.

In a skillet, melt the butter and sauté the onion, cooking until translucent. (Do not let the onion brown.) Add flour and stir, cooking for 5 minutes to form a roux or white sauce. Add 2 cups of the chicken broth from the pot of potatoes. Stir frequently. If there are lumps, add more liquid and pour into a food processor. Blend until smooth and creamy.

Remove potatoes from the chicken broth and set aside. Bring the broth to a boil, and then remove from heat. Add the instant potatoes and blend thoroughly. Slowly add the half-and-half, stirring constantly. Return the pot to the stove and cook 10 minutes on medium low heat (do not let boil). Add the flour mixture to the pot and stir with a whisk. If you want the soup to be thicker, puree some of the cooked potatoes in a blender and add them to the soup.

Return the cooked potatoes to the creamy mixture in the pot. Add salt and pepper to taste.

Top with grated cheddar cheese or bacon bits and serve.

Tip: The soup will thicken as it stands.

FRESH SUMMER SQUASH POTLUCK CASSEROLE (GLUTEN FREE)

Ingredients

4 cups sliced yellow
    squash

1 large white onion,
    sliced

1 cup sour cream

2 large eggs

½ tsp. salt

½ tsp. pepper

2 cups shredded
    cheddar cheese

When we were first married, we lived in a tiny apartment that had a small patch of ground outside the back door. To help save cash we decided to plant a small garden. The squash outgrew all other veggies and yielded a bountiful harvest. We'll never forget when our friends, Jim and Katherine Brown, invited their Sunday school class members to a potluck dinner and upon arrival we discovered we weren't the only ones who had grown a crop of squash. The table was covered with assorted styles of squash casseroles. Gratefully, our hosts had provided the meat and bread. Here's what we contributed to the unforgettable collection of squash-ness.

Directions

Preheat oven to 350°.

Prepare a 9 x 13-inch baking dish (or similar size) sprayed with a nonstick cooking spray.

Add squash and onion to a large saucepan, cover with water, and cook until tender. Remove from heat and drain in a colander. Place cooked squash and onion in the casserole dish.

In a separate bowl, combine sour cream, eggs, salt, and pepper and pour over squash and onion mixture.

Top with cheddar cheese.

Bake 25 to 30 minutes, or until bubbly and golden brown.

ETHEL'S EFFORTLESS SQUASH DRESSING

Ingredients

2 cups cooked, drained, and
    smashed squash

2 cups cubed cornbread

1 onion, chopped

1 (10.5 oz.) can cream of chicken soup

2 eggs, beaten

1 stick butter, melted

Directions

Preheat oven to 350°. Mix all ingredients and place in a 9 x 13-inch baking dish. Bake for 25 minutes.

CABBAGE CASSEROLE

Ingredients

Nonstick cooking spray

½ medium head cabbage, chopped

1 medium size onion, chopped

⅓ cup oil (organic coconut oil works well)

1 (10.5 oz.) can mushroom soup

½ cup milk

⅔ cup sour cream

2 cups shredded cheddar cheese

Salt and pepper

This recipe can be used with potatoes but if a lower carb intake is preferred, cabbage is an excellent alternative.

Directions

Preheat oven to 350°.

Grease a 9 x 9-inch casserole dish with nonstick spray.

Place cabbage, onion, and oil in large skillet and sauté on medium heat until soft.

In a mixing bowl combine cream of mushroom soup, milk, and sour cream. Season with salt and pepper.

Combine all ingredients into mixing bowl then pour into casserole dish.

Top with cheddar cheese.

Bake for 30 minutes or until cheese is golden brown and bubbly.

Serves 6 to 8

MOM'S MOREL MUSHROOMS

Ingredients

1 lb. morel mushrooms

¼ cup cooking oil

½ cup flour

1 tsp. salt

½ tsp. pepper

My (Steve) mom and my brother, Ney Jr., loved to hunt morel mushrooms each spring. They seemed to have an internal sonar system that led them to the edible fungi. I accompanied the two of them on many occasions, trying my best to find the hidden delicacies, but I usually came home with an empty sack. While the umbrella-shaped mushrooms are a gastronomical treat, unless you're an expert at identifying mushrooms, don't pick them yourself. Some mushrooms that closely resemble morels are poisonous.

Directions

Slice open each mushroom lengthwise and rinse well. Cut away the woody stub at the bottom of the stem. Be careful to handle the mushrooms as little as possible because they are quite delicate.

Add enough oil to a skillet to cover the bottom. Heat to hot, but not burning.

Turn each mushroom in a mixture of flour, salt, and pepper. Shake off the excess and gently place in skillet. Cook mushrooms until golden brown, turning once.

Remove from skillet and place on paper towels to drain. Serve hot, if possible.

SUMMER FRESH SALAD

Ingredients

10 oz. romaine lettuce

½ cup sliced fresh strawberries

½ cup fresh blueberries

½ cup canned mandarin oranges, drained

1 fresh apple, sliced or diced

¼ cup chopped pecans

½ cup feta cheese

Directions

Combine all ingredients.

Toss with poppy seed dressing (below) to desired taste.

POPPY SEED DRESSING

Ingredients

¼ cup white wine vinegar

¼ cup granulated sugar

1 small onion, grated (use small side of grater)

1½ T. poppy seeds

½ tsp. salt

½ tsp. ground mustard

2 tsp. mayonnaise

½ cup olive oil

Directions

In a small bowl, whisk the white wine vinegar and sugar until smooth.

Add onion, poppy seeds, salt, and ground mustard.

Whisk until well combined.

Whisking dressing continuously, slowly pour olive oil into dressing.

Mix thoroughly.

Pour dressing into airtight container or jar and store in refrigerator.

Shake before using to re-combine ingredients

JAN'S CUCUMBER SALAD

BY JAN LEARY

Ingredients

1 lb. cucumber, thinly sliced

1½ tsp. sugar

½ tsp. kosher salt

2½ T. red wine vinegar

½ cup cherry tomatoes, sliced in half

½ small onion, thinly sliced

Directions

In a medium bowl, toss sliced cucumbers with sugar and salt and let stand 5 to 10 minutes.

Stir in vinegar, tomatoes, and onion.

Cover and refrigerate at least 10 minutes.

Ready to serve!

KETO-FRIENDLY VEGGIE PIZZA

Ingredients

2 low-carb (Carb Balance) tortilla wraps

1 T. olive oil

1 bell pepper, diced

½ cup chopped red onion

1 cup loosely packed spinach leaves

½ cup chopped tomato

½ cup sliced mushrooms

⅓ cup pizza or marinara sauce

1 cup shredded mozzarella cheese

This is one of our favorite guilt-free ways to use fresh picked (or purchased) veggies!

Note: The amount of ingredients shown can vary according to how "loaded" you want the pizza to be.

Directions

Preheat oven to 400°. Place olive oil in a large skillet.

Under medium to high temperature, toast the tortilla wraps on both sides until lightly browned.

Place wraps on sheet and spread a thin layer of pizza sauce or marinara on each.

Top with veggies and cheese.

Bake 10 to 15 minutes or until cheese is bubbly and browned to your liking.

Allow to cool and serve.

ANNIE'S "ANGEL-ED" EGGS

Ingredients

6 eggs

2 T. salt

⅓ cup mayonnaise

1 tsp. prepared mustard

Salt and pepper

Paprika

Our grandkids prefer to call this side-dish treat "angel-ed" eggs. They are an expected part of every big family meal.

Directions

Place eggs in saucepan and cover with cold water a minimum of half an inch above eggs.

Add salt to water. The salt makes the egg shells more brittle which makes peeling easier.

Bring to a full boil then put a lid on the saucepan and turn heat off. Allow eggs to remain undisturbed for 10 minutes.

Peel the eggs and cut lengthwise, remove the yolk and place yolks in a bowl.

Add mayo and mustard in the bowl. Season with salt and pepper and mix until smooth.

Fill the egg white halves with yolk mixture and sprinkle with paprika.

Fruit Salads

FRUIT CHIPOTLE CHUTNEY

Ingredients

4 cups fruit, fresh or frozen

2 T. chipotle peppers in adobo sauce, finely chopped (the more peppers, the spicier the chutney)

1 cup finely chopped apple

½ cup white vinegar

⅓ cup honey

⅓ cup white sugar

3 T. mustard seeds

½ tsp. salt

½ tsp. ground ginger

Directions

Mix all ingredients in a pan. Cook, uncovered, on the stove at medium heat for approximately 25 minutes or until thickened.

Remove from stove and allow to cool.

Store in an airtight container and place in the refrigerator.

Optional: Place in a food processor and puree for a few seconds until slightly smooth.

CREAMY FRUIT SALAD

Ingredients

¾ cup sugar

1 (8 oz.) pkg. cream cheese

1 (12 oz.) pkg. frozen strawberries

1 (8 oz.) tub Cool Whip

1 (10 oz.) can crushed pineapple, drained

2 large bananas, sliced into rounds

1 cup mini marshmallows

½ cup nuts (optional)

Directions

Whip sugar and cream cheese together. Add remaining ingredients. Chill and serve.

FRESH FRUIT SALAD

Ingredients

2 cups diced apples (with or without peel)

1 cup sliced bananas, not too ripe

1 cup grapes (white, red, or combination)

1 cup diced peaches (fresh, or canned and drained)

1 cup roughly chopped oranges (or canned mandarin oranges, drained and cut into pieces)

1 cup chopped strawberries (fresh or frozen)

½ cup coconut, toasted and shredded

Directions

Mix all fruit in a large bowl.

Just before serving, sprinkle toasted, shredded coconut on top.

Tip: Any fruit you enjoy will be great in this salad, so be creative.

Breads

MOM'S BISCUITS

SUBMITTED BY ALICE CLICK

My husband, Karl, thinks it's funny when I explain how to make Mom's special biscuits that we call "Sylvie Biscuits." It's hard to give a recipe for something I just do, but here it is.

Mix the flour, butter, and milk together. Now, you have to put enough milk in there, but not too much. Work the dough, but not too long.

I use canola oil and bake the biscuits in a square, glass baking dish. I think this really makes a difference in how they turn out. Preheat the glass dish. This is the key to getting the biscuits to rise quickly. Because Mom would preheat her biscuit pan with a scoop of Crisco melting in it, that's what I do.

She would take the biscuit dough that had been cut into large, round shapes (if you don't have a biscuit cutter you can use the top of a glass dipped in flour) and flop each biscuit individually into the hot grease. Then she placed it in the hot oven. This caused the biscuit to have a brown, crunchy bottom. Mom loved to take the bottom of the biscuit and dip it into her coffee. I can see her doing it as I write this. She always made everything look so yummy. I bake them just like I would a cake: 350 degrees—at least in my oven. Yours may need to be 400 degrees.

If you'd like more conventional instructions…

SYLVIE BISCUITS

Ingredients

2 cups self-rising flour

⅓ cup cold butter

¾ cup milk or buttermilk

Additional flour for rolling out the biscuits

Crisco shortening or nonstick cooking spray

Directions

Preheat oven to 400°. Place the self-rising flour in a large bowl. Cut in the butter until the mixture resembles coarse crumbs. Stir in milk until the flour mixture is moistened.

Turn the biscuit dough onto a lightly floured surface. Using additional flour to keep the dough from sticking to the surface, roll the dough to a ½-inch thickness. Cut out the desired biscuit size and place on a lightly greased cookie sheet.

Bake for 8 to 10 minutes or until golden brown.

Serve warm!

CORNBREAD

Ingredients

1 (8.5 oz.) pkg. Jiffy corn muffin mix

3 eggs

¼ cup vegetable oil

½ cup sour cream

¼ cup sugar

Directions

Preheat oven to 350°. Ignore package instructions. Instead, stir muffin mix, eggs, oil, sour cream, and sugar together. Pour into a greased 9-inch pan or cast-iron skillet.

Bake for 20 minutes or until a toothpick inserted in the center pulls out cleanly.

DOROTHY KELLY'S MEXICAN CORNBREAD

Ingredients

1½ cups self-rising cornmeal

1 (8 oz.) carton sour cream

1 (8 ½ oz.) can creamed style corn soup

2 eggs

⅓ cup cooking oil

2 cups shredded mild cheddar cheese

2 jalapeño peppers, chopped

Directions

Preheat oven 350°. Mix all ingredients together.

Pour into 9-inch pan or cast-iron skillet.

Bake for about 40 minutes or until golden brown.

BANANA BREAD

Ingredients

½ cup honey

½ cup vegetable oil

2 eggs, beaten

3 ripe bananas, mashed

2 cups self-rising flour

1 tsp. baking soda

3 T. milk

½ tsp. vanilla

½ cup chopped walnuts or pecans

Directions

Beat honey and oil together. Add eggs and banana and beat well. Add flour, baking soda, milk, and vanilla. Mix thoroughly. Add nuts and stir.

Bake in a loaf pan or muffin tins at 350° for approximately 1 hour or until solid and brown.

A TASTE OF PARADISE PUMPKIN/CRANBERRY BREAD

Ingredients

2 cups self-rising flour

2 cups sugar

1 tsp. soda

2 tsp. cinnamon

2 tsp. nutmeg

1 tsp. ground cloves

1 cup oil

4 eggs

1 (15 oz.) can pure pumpkin

1 cup dried cranberries

Directions

Preheat oven to 350°.

Combine and mix all ingredients except cranberries. After mixing, add cranberries.

Pour into two greased and floured loaf pans (or one greased and floured Bundt pan).

Bake for 30 to 35 minutes or until a toothpick comes out clean.

ZUCCHINI BREAD

Ingredients

Nonstick cooking spray

3 cups self-rising flour (or 3 cups all-purpose flour, ¼ tsp. baking powder, and 1 tsp. salt)

1 tsp. baking soda

3 T. cinnamon

3 eggs

3 T. vanilla

2¼ cups sugar

1 cup oil

3 cups grated zucchini (include skin and juice)

1 cup chopped walnuts (or pecans)

This is a great way to get your kids to eat a vegetable they might otherwise refuse to try. By the end of the summer, with my garden overrun by zucchini, I look for all kinds of ways to use this squash.

Directions

Lightly grease 3 medium-size loaf pans.

Sift flour, baking soda, and cinnamon into a large bowl. Add other ingredients and mix well.

Bake at 350° for 1 hour.

Hush Puppies...

REQUIRED WITH CATFISH!

L egend has it that hush puppies originated in the Civil War days. Southerners would sit around the campfire preparing their supper. If they'd heard that Yankees were near, they would toss their dogs some of the fried cakes and command "Hush, puppies!" to keep them quiet. I (Annie) don't know if that's true, but it sure makes a lot of sense…and it's a fun story.

Our family has always enjoyed the tasty round bites. And we're especially fond of the ones we used to get when we lived close to a "greasy spoon" that specialized in fried catfish, hush puppies, and coleslaw. I'm not sure how our arteries survived (perhaps we had youth on our side), but we loved to go to Captain Paulo's Catfish Diner and eat our fill.

CHAPMAN'S CHIN-LICKIN'-GOOD HUSH PUPPIES

Ingredients

Cooking oil, enough to
   reach 2-inch depth
   in pot
2 cups finely ground
   white cornmeal
   (if you use self-rising
   cornmeal, omit
   baking soda and salt)
1 T. sugar
2 tsp. baking soda
2 tsp. salt
1 T. minced yellow onion
1 egg
1 cup buttermilk
4½ T. cold water
Jalapenos or mild
   chilies, chopped
   (optional)

This recipe isn't the original from Captain Paulo's, but after many attempts my family agrees it's close enough to be delicious and a family favorite.

Directions

Heat cooking oil to 365° in a deep fat fryer or deep, heavy pot.

Put the cornmeal in a large mixing bowl.

In a small bowl, mix the sugar, baking soda, salt, and onion. Add the egg and buttermilk, and beat until foamy. Pour all at once into the cornmeal and stir lightly to mix. Add just enough cold water to make the dough the right consistency for dropping into oil. If desired, stir in jalapenos to taste. (The dough should be thick enough to drop from the spoon slowly but easily.)

Using a tablespoon, drop one ball at a time into the hot oil. Fry each one for 2 to 3 minutes or until golden brown. Keep turning the "puppies" until all sides are evenly brown.

Remove from oil and place on paper towels to drain. Place hush puppies, uncovered, in warm oven until you're ready to serve.

Tip: You won't want to serve this every day, but why not treat your family to this special treat every once in a while? Be sure to take a nice long walk as a family as soon as everyone can pry themselves off the couch.

Muffins

BLUEBERRIES GALORE

One of the tasty highlights of summer is the homegrown blueberries that we handpick at a nearby, self-serve grove. We like to arrive early in the day or later in the afternoon to avoid the midday heat and allow enough time to gather 3 to 4 gallons of berries.

Back at home we wash and de-bug the first pint and enjoy them raw or as a topping on cereal, yogurt, or ice cream—and especially as an added treat in pancakes. The rest of the blueberries are prepared for freezing for later use. Here's how we do it…

First, we don't wash the berries before freezing to avoid freezer burn and clumping. We wash them after thawing.

Using a large cookie tray, pour enough berries to cover the surface but only one berry deep.

Carefully inspect and remove any bugs (ants, worms, little spiders, etc.), stems, and any foreign debris. (A slick-sided, narrow-mouth Mason jar is good for holding the bugs and anything else removed).

Place berries in a freezer-friendly ziplock bag. Typically, a pint of berries per bag is good. This amount eliminates waste after thawing if all the contents of the bag are not immediately used. Remove as much air as possible and seal. Using an indelible marker, put the package date on the bag.

When the hankering for blueberries hits, remove a package from the freezer and let them slow-thaw in the fridge.

Enjoy the taste and the benefits of your own, handpicked blueberries!

BEST EVER BLUEBERRY MUFFINS

Ingredients

1 egg

1 cup buttermilk (or regular milk with 1 T. white vinegar and let stand 5 minutes)

¼ cup oil

⅔ cup sugar

1 tsp. cinnamon

1 tsp. lemon juice

½ tsp. vanilla

2 cups self-rising flour

1½ cups blueberries

Directions

Preheat oven at 350°.

Combine wet ingredients in a large bowl. Add flour, mix gently, and then fold in blueberries.

Pour mixture into greased muffin pan. Bake 20 to 24 minutes.

Makes 12 muffins.

FRESH PEACH MUFFINS

Ingredients

Nonstick cooking spray or paper muffin cups

1 egg

1 cup milk

¼ cup shortening, melted (or cooking oil)

⅔ cup sugar

¼ tsp. vanilla

½ tsp. salt

¼ tsp. cinnamon

1 tsp. lemon juice

2 cups all-purpose flour

2 tsp. baking powder

1 cup (overflowing) chopped fresh peaches (unpeeled)

Directions

Preheat oven to 350°. Grease muffin tins or have paper baking cups ready in muffin tins.

Beat the egg, and then stir in milk, shortening, sugar, vanilla, salt, cinnamon, and lemon juice.

Sift together the flour and baking powder, and then stir into milk mixture until just blended. Don't overmix. Fold in peaches. Pour into muffin cups, approximately two-thirds full.

Bake until lightly brown and firm, approximately 12 to 15 minutes.

Part Six

DESSERTS

Pies and Cobblers

No meal is quite complete
without the taste of something sweet!

This little poem may be short in words, but it's long on truth. Hardly anything puts an exclamation point on a great meal of wild game than a tantalizing treat. But I'm (Steve) reminded of a remark Annie's mother, Sylvia, the youngest of her Grandma Naomi's six children, made one day. Her words remind us of what it means to truly love others. She said,

> I grew up thinking my mom didn't like apple pie because so many times I saw her give her slice to others to eat, especially our visitors. I didn't realize until I was older that what gave her more pleasure than the sweetness of the pie was the smile on someone else's face when they were enjoying it.

ANNIE'S APPLE PIE

Ingredients

Pie Shells

2 cups all-purpose flour, sifted

1 tsp. salt

4 T. butter

6 T. Crisco shortening

6 T. milk

Pie Filling

1 cup sugar

2 T. all-purpose flour

1 tsp. ground cinnamon

½ tsp. ground nutmeg

Dash of salt

6 to 8 apples, pared, cored, and thinly sliced or grated (approximately 6 cups)

2 T. cold butter, chopped into tiny pieces

Directions

Pie Shells

In a medium bowl, sift together the flour and salt. Cut in shortening and butter with a pastry blender. Add milk and gently stir with fork until well mixed. (Add more flour if needed for best consistency.)

Divide in half to form two balls. Sprinkle flour on counter or bread board. Place each dough ball on the counter, and roll out to form round circles slightly larger than the pie plate.

Place one circle on the pie plate and gently conform the dough to the plate. The other one will go on top of pie filling.

Pie Filling

In a large bowl, combine sugar, flour, spices, and salt. Add apples and mix until apples are well covered.

Place the apple mixture in the pie pan over the pastry shell. Dot apples with butter.

Add the top pie shell, and cut slits so the steam can escape. Crimp the pie shell edges together to seal. Sprinkle top with sugar.

Bake at 400° for 50 minutes or until pie crust is a golden brown.

A SIMPLY DELICIOUS PLEASURE

In addition to Annie's delightful desserts that will satisfy our sweet tooth, we want to include a recipe that I (Steve) enjoy—and willingly drive several hours from home to consume.

For the past few years I've been privileged to hunt in Indiana with my friend Don Hicks. I deeply value the "therapy" of our fellowship and the chasing critters we do in his part of the world. But there's another reason I show up at his door. I know that when I arrive, more than likely there'll be a fresh batch of his wife's fried pies waiting for me on the kitchen counter. Doris has mastered the creation of this delectable treat. And let me tell you, there's absolutely nothing like pouring a hot cup of herb tea sweetened with honey from a Thermos and unwrapping one or two of Doris's fried pies while sitting in a deer stand on a cold November morning. The combination makes me really glad I'm alive... and visiting Indiana!

Doris has graciously agreed to share her recipe with our family and yours.

DORIS'S LIP-SMACKIN' FRIED PIES

Ingredients

2 T. butter

½ cup cooking oil

1 can Pillsbury Grands biscuits
   (or similar)

16 oz. applesauce or apple butter*

Directions

In a large skillet, heat oil and butter on medium-high.

Open biscuits and roll each one out to about a ¼ -inch thick.

Put a quarter cup apple filling on one half of a biscuit, fold it over to make a pie, and press the edges together with a fork to seal.

Slide biscuits into the skillet and cook until golden brown. Turn them and brown other side. Remove and drain on layers of paper towels.

Repeat until all pies are done.

* If you don't have homemade apple butter, spice up the applesauce by adding 1 teaspoon cinnamon, ½ teaspoon nutmeg, and ¼ teaspoon cloves. Feel free to add more of these spices until you get the taste you desire.

OLD-FASHIONED CUSTARD PIE

Ingredients

1 cup sugar

4 T. flour

1 cup boiling water

1 egg

1 tsp. lemon extract

3 T. cider vinegar

1 pie shell, baked

Directions

In a pan, mix sugar and flour together. Add boiling water, stir, and cook for 5 minutes on medium heat.

Beat the egg and add to the sugar mixture. Cook for 2 minutes, and then add the lemon and vinegar. Cook, stirring constantly, until a smooth, pudding consistency.

Pour the mixture into the pie shell. Let cool and serve. Refrigerate leftovers—if there are any!

PERFECT PEACH COBBLER

Ingredients

1 (16 oz.) can sliced peaches, drained

1 cup milk

1 cup sugar

1 cup self-rising flour

1 stick butter, melted

Directions

Preheat oven to 350°. In a large bowl, combine all ingredients except the butter. Mix slightly (it's okay if there are lumps).

Melt the butter in a loaf pan or square baking dish by placing it in the oven for a few minutes. Remove pan and carefully pour the peach concoction into the melted butter.

Bake for 50 minutes or until done. The edges should be a deep, golden brown. Make sure the crust in the middle is done.

Cakes

QUICK AND EASY CHEESECAKE

Ingredients

2 (8 oz.) pkgs. cream cheese

⅔ cup sugar

8 oz. sour cream

2 tsp. vanilla

16 oz. Cool Whip

2 graham cracker pie crusts, already
   prepared

1 (12 oz.) can cherry pie filling

Directions

In a large bowl, mix cream cheese, sugar, sour cream, and vanilla. Beat with an electric mixer until smooth.

Gently fold in the Cool Whip.

Pour into the pie crust pans and chill in the refrigerator for 1 hour.

Remove from refrigerator, top with pie filling, and serve.

AUNT BESSIE'S CARROT CAKE

Ingredients

4 eggs

¾ cup oil

2 cups sugar

2 cups all-purpose flour

½ tsp. cinnamon

½ tsp. salt

2 tsp. soda

3 cups grated carrots

1 cup chopped nuts
   (pecans or walnuts)

Directions

Preheat oven to 350°. Beat eggs, oil, and sugar in a large bowl. Sift dry ingredients in a medium-size bowl. Combine carrots and nuts and stir in a bit of dry ingredients and then add remaining dry ingredients to sugar mixture. Gently fold in carrots and nuts.

Prepare pan with oil and flour on sides and parchment paper on bottom.

Bake in 9 x 13-inch pan for 40 minutes.

Top with Cream Cheese Icing (below).

CREAM CHEESE ICING

Ingredients

1 stick butter

8 oz. cream cheese

3 cups powdered sugar

1 tsp. vanilla

Directions

Mix all ingredients with an electric mixer until smooth and fluffy.

PERFECTO POUND CAKE

Ingredients

2 sticks butter, room temperature

3 cups sugar

5 eggs, room temperature

½ cup sour cream

2 T. vanilla

3 cups cake flour (if cake flour not available, whisk all-purpose flour until fluffy)

½ tsp. baking soda

Directions

Preheat oven to 350°.

Prepare 2 loaf pans, buttered and floured. Cream butter and sugar in a large mixing bowl.

Add eggs one at a time while continuing to mix on low setting with hand mixer or stand mixer.

Add sour cream and vanilla, and continue mixing for 30 seconds.

Combine flour and baking soda and add to egg mixture 1 cup at a time, continuing to mix on medium speed for 1 to 2 minutes until flour is incorporated.

Pour into the prepared loaf pans and bake for 45 minutes or until a toothpick comes out clean. Be careful not to overbake.

Serve with Fresh Fruit Topping (below).

FRESH FRUIT TOPPING

Ingredients

1 cup chopped fresh strawberries

1 peach, chopped

1 cup blueberries

½ cup thinly sliced pineapple chunks

½ banana, chopped

2 T. fresh lemon juice

This recipe can be made with any combination of your favorite fruits. Here is one of our favorites.

Directions

Combine all ingredients in a bowl except lemon juice.

Sprinkle lemon juice evenly over fruit to keep it from turning brown.

Heap topping on the pound cake and add Cool Whip for an extra zing if desired.

EASTER'S DELICIOUS APPLE CAKE

Steve's late grandmother, Easter Daisy Chapman, wife of the late George Stonewall Chapman and mother of 11 children, was known throughout Logan County, West Virginia, for her wonderful apple cake. Unfortunately, as far as we know, her recipe was never written down. But that doesn't stop the entire Chapman Clan from doing their best to duplicate the unbelievably delicious cake.

Every time I bake anything connected with apples and sugar, my mind goes back to that cake. I've come to believe the elusive ingredient that no one can figure out was probably the generous scoop of love that only Easter could offer.

Here's an apple cake recipe that I respectfully call "It's Almost Easter's Apple Cake."

IT'S ALMOST EASTER'S APPLE CAKE

Ingredients

1½ cups sugar

1 cup vegetable oil

2 eggs

2 cups all-purpose flour

1 tsp. baking soda

1 tsp. vanilla

¼ tsp. nutmeg

1 tsp. cinnamon or apple pie spice

½ tsp. salt

3 cups thinly sliced tart apples

Whipped cream (optional)

Directions

Preheat oven to 350°. Grease a 9 x 13-inch baking pan.

Mix sugar, oil, and eggs until blended. Beat 1 minute. Stir in remaining ingredients except apples. Beat 1 minute. Stir in apples.

Bake for 35 to 45 minutes or until wooden toothpick inserted comes out clean.

Tip: This cake doesn't need icing, but it tastes great with a generous dollop of whipped cream.

Candies

MILK AND HONEY BALLS

Ingredients

1¼ cups honey

1½ cups peanut butter

3 cups dry powdered skim milk

Directions

Mix honey and peanut butter. Gradually add dry milk, mixing well.

With greased hands, form dough into small balls. Roll the balls in additional milk powder.

Chill until firm and serve.

GRANDMA'S MOLASSES CANDY

Ingredients

2 cups molasses

1 cup sugar

1 T. vinegar

Pinch of baking soda

3 cups chopped black walnuts

Nonstick cooking spray

Directions

In a large saucepan, combine molasses, sugar, and vinegar. Cook on low heat until crunchy or brittle when a little is dropped into cold water. The candy thermometer should reach 260°.

Stir in baking soda and nuts.

Pour into greased pan and let set, approximately 5 minutes or until cool.

Break into pieces when cold and serve.

HEAVENLY KISSES

Ingredients

2 egg whites

½ cup fine, granulated sugar, divided

½ tsp. vanilla

Directions

Preheat oven to 250°. Beat egg whites until stiff and dry. Beat in 6 tablespoons of sugar, a spoonful at a time, and then beat until peaks form.

Add vanilla and then fold in the rest of the sugar.

Spoon onto cookie sheet and form into "kiss" shape.

Bake for 50 minutes.

Cookies and Brownies

NINE MILE BLACK WALNUT COOKIES

Ingredients

½ cup butter

6 T. brown sugar

6 T. granulated sugar

1 egg (free range if available)

1 tsp. vanilla

1 ¼ cups self-rising flour

½ tsp. baking soda

1 cup chopped black walnuts

One sweet memory of the old farm on Nine Mile Creek in West Virginia, where I (Annie) was raised, was seeing the black walnuts in the gravel driveway. They were placed there intentionally for a very practical reason—to let the truck and tractor tires peel away the outer shell so that we wouldn't have to do it by hand, thus avoiding the nearly permanent yellow stain that fresh-fallen walnuts would leave on our hands. Smart move!

Directions

Preheat oven to 375°. In a large bowl, cream butter and sugars until light. Beat in egg and vanilla.

Sift flour and baking soda together in a medium size bowl and then add to the butter mixture. Gently combine and then fold in nuts. Drop dough from teaspoon onto ungreased sheet.

Bake for 10 minutes. Makes 2½ dozen cookies.

GLUTEN-FREE PEANUT BUTTER COOKIES

Ingredients

1 stick butter, room temperature

½ cup creamy or chunky peanut butter

½ cup granulated sugar

½ cup brown sugar

1 egg

½ tsp. vanilla

1¼ cups blanched almond flour

¼ tsp. salt

½ tsp. baking powder

½ tsp. baking soda

Directions

Preheat oven to 375°. Cream butter, peanut butter, sugars, egg, and vanilla.

Sift together the flour, salt, baking powder, and baking soda. Blend into creamed mixture.

Shape into 1-inch balls and place 2 inches apart on ungreased cookie sheet.

Dip a fork in water and compress each ball to desired shape.

Bake for 10 to 12 minutes. Makes approximately 2 dozen cookies.

"LITTLE FRIENDS" CHOCOLATE CHIP COOKIES

Ingredients

2 cups butter or Butter Crisco

2 cups brown sugar

2 cups sugar

4 eggs

2 tsp. vanilla

4 cups self-rising flour

5 cups quick oats

2 tsp. baking soda

3 cups chocolate chips

3 cups chopped walnuts (optional)

I (Steve) am an avid hunter who also enjoys the game of golf. As I often say, I like to hunt and play golf because in doing both I get to go to the woods and look for something! I usually meet my regular golf group at the first tee box with a batch of Annie's chocolate chip cookies to share with my "little friends" (as Annie calls them). They love them and Annie graciously keeps them coming. This recipe makes lots of cookies known to inspire birdies and eagles…or provide consolation for those bogies and double bogies.

Directions

Preheat oven to 375°. Cream together the butter, both sugars, eggs, and vanilla. Mix in the flour and baking soda until well combined. Stir in the oatmeal and chocolate chips.

Spoon rounded spoonfuls of dough onto a cookie sheet, 2 inches apart.

Bake for approximately 6 minutes or until lightly brown.

GLUTEN-FREE SHOOTIN' HOUSE BROWNIES

THANKS TO KAREN FLETCHER FOR THIS TREAT!

Ingredients

1 cup butter, melted (or melted
    margarine or Butter-Flavor Crisco)

2 cups sugar

2 tsp. vanilla

4 eggs

⅓ cup cocoa

1½ cups blanched almond flour

2 tsp. baking powder

¼ tsp. salt

¼ tsp. baking soda

2 T. (heaping) peanut butter

Directions

Preheat oven to 350°. Combine butter and sugar, mix until smooth. Add vanilla and eggs and mix. Add cocoa, flour, baking powder, salt, and baking soda and gently combine. Stir in peanut butter. Pour into a 9 x 9-inch greased pan.

Bake for 45 to 50 minutes or until a knife comes out clean.

Ice Cream

GLUTEN-FREE AND SUGAR-FREE STRAWBERRY ICE CREAM

Ingredients

4 cups frozen, whole strawberries

2 cups whipping cream

1 cup water

1 T. vanilla

Directions

Place ingredients in a blender and blend until creamy and smooth.

Enjoy as is or topped with chopped nuts of choice, chocolate syrup, or other sweet additions.

Serves 4.

Toppings

GOOD NEIGHBOR'S FRIED APPLES

Ingredients

2 to 3 lbs. apples

4 oz. (½ stick) butter

¾ cup sugar

2 T. cinnamon

2 tsp. nutmeg

Dash of salt

¼ cup all-purpose flour

Our neighbors have four apple trees and every year at least three of them are laden with baseball-size fruit. Thankfully, they happily share their bounty with us. Along with the obvious use of the apples in Annie's Apple Pie (see page 172), this recipe makes a delicious topping for cheesecake, pancakes, and other desserts.

Directions

Gather, peel, core (de-worm if necessary), and thinly slice as many apples as a large skillet can hold.

Melt butter in the skillet on medium to low heat.

Add prepared apple slices.

Sprinkle the sugar, cinnamon, nutmeg, salt, and flour onto the apples, then stir and continue to cook until the apples are tender. You can add more or less spices and sugar to your preferred taste. Use the fried apples as a pie filling or as a topping.

GRANNY'S GRANOLA

Ingredients

7 cups regular rolled oats

½ cup shredded coconut (or small flakes)

½ cup raw pepitas

½ cup raw, hulled sunflower seeds

½ cup raw sesame seeds

¾ cup white wheat flour (if freshly ground, no need to add wheat germ or bran)

½ cup ground flaxseed

½ cup chopped almonds

½ cup chopped walnuts

½ tsp. cinnamon

½ cup olive oil

1 cup honey or maple syrup

1 tsp. vanilla

Directions

Preheat oven to 350°. Mix together the dry ingredients thoroughly. Warm the oil and honey and combine all wet ingredients, then add to the dry ingredients and mix all together.

Put mixture on 2 to 3 cookie sheets sprayed with oil and bake 10 minutes.

Perfect by itself or as a topping for yogurt, ice cream or great with milk. Add dried cranberries for extra sweetness.

CHARLES AND PATSY'S HAND-PICKED BLACKBERRY SYRUP

Ingredients

3 cups fresh blackberries, de-bugged and washed

1 cup granulated sugar

1 cup water

Our neighbors, Charles and Patsy, live along our walking route and have a blackberry patch that annually yields juicy, thumb-size blackberries each year. We're grateful for the times we've walked by their house and heard Charles say, "Hey, neighbor…want some blackberries?" Usually we head home with around a quart of berries and besides eating them raw we use them for making syrup that we can put on pancakes, ice cream, or other desserts.

Directions

Add blackberries, sugar, and water to a medium saucepan over medium heat.

Bring to a boil, then continue boiling for 2 minutes while stirring occasionally.

Remove from heat and remove seeds by pouring through a fine mesh strainer.

Store in an airtight container up to 14 days.

Makes 2 cups.

Part Seven

GRAVIES, MARINADES, & SAUCES

Gravies

POOR MAN'S GRAVY

Ingredients

3 T. bacon drippings, grease,
    shortening, or lard (or 3 T. oil)
¼ cup plus 1 T. all-purpose flour
1 cup milk or water
½ tsp. salt
½ tsp. pepper

Directions

In a cast-iron skillet heat the bacon drippings to hot, but not burning. Stirring as you go, pour small amounts of flour into the grease and cook until the flour turns a nice brown. (Remember, it's easier to add more than to take away.)

Slowly pour milk into the flour mixture. Add as much liquid as you need to achieve the desired consistency of gravy. Add salt and pepper to taste and serve hot.

Tip: Sylvie Biscuits (page 163) taste delicious with this gravy. Let this gravy and biscuit combination remind you of the principles of simplicity…when we work hard and are grateful for what we have. Consider the difference between "making a killing" and "making a living," and remember that a good day is going to sleep with a full belly and a clear conscience.

TOMATO GRAVY

Ingredients

1 qt. canned, whole tomatoes
2 T. all-purpose flour
½ tsp. salt
½ cup cream
2 cups milk
2 T. butter
2 T. sugar

Directions

Place the tomatoes, including juice, in a saucepan and bring to a boil.

In a separate bowl, blend the flour and salt with the cream. Add the milk and stir.

Pour mixture into the boiling tomatoes, stirring constantly until mixture is thick.

Remove from heat. Stir in butter and sugar. Pour over hot biscuits and serve.

Tip: Sylvie Biscuits (page 163) are great with this recipe.

Brining Solution

LINDSEY'S BRINING SOLUTION

Ingredients

½ cup kosher salt

¼ cup sugar

Thyme

Rosemary

Crushed juniper berries

Directions

Add salt and sugar to a large bowl of water. You may also add any fresh (not dried) herbs, such as thyme and rosemary. Crushed juniper berries are a good addition too. Put the meat into the brine and let it sit in the refrigerator for 2 to 3 hours for smaller cuts of meat.

Marinades

ANNIE'S FAVORITE MARINADE

Ingredients

1 T. Worcestershire sauce

1 tsp. cumin

1 tsp. paprika

1 tsp. cayenne pepper

2 tsp. apple cider vinegar

Salt and pepper to taste

Directions

Mix everything together. If you need to, use a little more Worcestershire sauce so all the other ingredients blend well. The marinade needs to be thick enough to stay on the meat.

LEMON MARINADE

Ingredients

1 lemon

⅓ cup golden raisins

3 T. fresh lemon juice

1½ tsp. balsamic vinegar

1 tsp. salt

½ cup olive oil

2 T. capers, drained

Directions

Carefully peel lemon, being careful to avoid the white part of the rind, which is extremely bitter. Cut peel into ½-inch strips and set aside.

Soak raisins in boiling water for 5 minutes. Drain and set aside.

In a small bowl, whisk together lemon juice, balsamic vinegar, and salt. Gradually pour olive oil into mixture, whisking to emulsify (thicken). Stir in lemon zest strips, raisins, and capers.

MULTI-MEAT MARINADE

Ingredients

¼ cup cooking oil

1 cup chopped onion

1 cup chopped celery

1 cup chopped carrot

8 cups vinegar

4 cups water

1 T. allspice berries

1 T. whole cloves

1 T. chopped basil

1 T. thyme

3 bay leaves

½ cup chopped parsley

1 T. peppercorns, crushed

6 garlic cloves, crushed

This marinade is useful for all kinds of game meats as well as beef.

Directions

Pour oil in a skillet and sauté the onion, celery, and carrot. Add the rest of the ingredients and simmer for 1 hour. Strain and cool.

LINDSEY'S MARINADE

Ingredients

¼ cup soy sauce

¼ cup olive oil

2 T. ketchup

2 T. red wine vinegar

2 T. minced garlic

1 T. freshly ground black pepper

Directions

Mix all ingredients and pour over red meat in a freezer bag. Let meat marinate for 6 to 8 hours, turning every now and then to make sure all of meat gets covered.

MAMA'S MERRY MARINADE

Ingredients

½ cup peanut oil

¾ cup soy sauce

¼ cup Worcestershire sauce

2 T. dry mustard

⅓ cup lemon juice

½ cup vinegar

5 garlic cloves, pressed and minced

This marinade is great on any red meat.

Directions

Mix together all ingredients and use on your favorite red meat.

PAPA'S PERFECT WILD GAME MARINADE

Ingredients

¼ cup fresh lime juice

½ cup beef broth

2 tsp. ground cumin

4 tsp. ground coriander

2 cloves garlic, finely chopped

½ tsp. salt

½ tsp. pepper

1¼ cup olive oil

This makes approximately 2 cups of marinade that is really great to use on meat and vegetables.

Directions

Mix all the ingredients except the oil in a blender. With the blender on low, slowly pour the oil in until everything is mixed well.

Cover and refrigerate until ready to use.

MY DEER'S BIGGER THAN YOURS MARINADE

Ingredients

½ cup cider or red wine vinegar

2 garlic cloves, minced

2 T. kosher salt

Cold water

This marinade is perfect for red meat or game birds.

Directions

In a large bowl, mix together all ingredients. Add the frozen or fresh meat and enough water to cover the meat. Soak overnight in the refrigerator.

VENISON MARINADE

Ingredients

¾ cup teriyaki sauce

2 T. red wine

3 cloves garlic, minced

¼ tsp. black pepper

This marinade can be used for any cut of venison except ground. Try this on the best of all venison cuts—backstrap tenderloin.

Directions

Rinse the venison in cold water and pat dry.

In a plastic ziplock bag, combine the desired amounts of teriyaki sauce, red wine, garlic, and black pepper. Don't add any extra salt since the teriyaki is salty already.

Whatever smells good to you will taste good. Let your nose be your guide.

Marinate the meat for 2 to 24 hours, depending on time available and size of cut (the bigger the cut, the longer the marinating time).

Spice Rubs

LET'S MAKE GARLIC POWDER

BY JAN LEARY

Why make your own garlic powder? Simple, because it has no preservatives, no anti-clumping agents, and the taste is better than anything you can purchase at your local grocery store.

1. Peel, wash, and place fresh garlic cloves in a bowl.
2. Slice the garlic into uniform pieces. For small amounts, slicing by hand is easier but slower than a food processor.
3. Place the pieces on the dehydrator mats, spacing them so there is good airflow for 8 to 14 hours drying time depending on the number of garlic cloves, their wetness, and the humidity level.
4. Set the dehydrator temperature to 130°. If using an oven, set the temperature to 125° and place garlic on a sheet covered with parchment paper. Oven-dried garlic might be faster because the lowest setting is typically higher than a dehydrator setting. Watch it carefully in an oven so it doesn't burn.
5. The fully dehydrated pieces should snap, not bend. If it bends, it is NOT DRY, so dehydrate it longer.
6. When the garlic is completely dry, place it in a jar for the CONDITIONING process. Fill the jar with your dried garlic, leaving an inch or so at the top. Put on the lid and set it on the counter for 7 to 10 days. Shake/flip/rotate it gently once every day. The pieces should flow freely. If you see any clumping or any moisture on the sides of the jar, then put it back into the dehydrator.
7. If you see MOLD, throw it away and start over. Mold seen on the jar from the outside is a sure sign that mold is in places you cannot see. Not worth the risk. Toss it!
8. After conditioning, powder the garlic in a food processor or coffee grinder. Powder only a small amount (as much as you would use for a few meals), leaving the rest in your airtight jar. The moisture that is absorbed by the garlic during opening/closing the container will cause it to clump a bit as this has none of the anti-caking agents and preservatives contained in store-bought garlic powder. You can try adding a few beans to the jar to reduce clumping. Store the powdered garlic in a cool dark place just as you would your other spices. Powder more from your dried, stored garlic reserves as needed.
9. Enjoy!

LINDSEY'S SPICE RUB

Ingredients

⅓ cup paprika

¼ cup sugar

3 T. black pepper

2 T. salt

2 tsp. dry mustard

2 tsp. cayenne pepper

1 tsp. white pepper

Directions

Mix all ingredients well and apply to meat.

DEE DEE'S DRY RUB

Ingredients

¼ cup garlic powder

3 T. black pepper

1 T. ground cumin

1 T. onion powder

4 T. paprika

2 T. chili powder

3 T. kosher salt

¼ cup brown sugar

This rub is great on any kind of wild game meat.

Directions

Mix all ingredients together. Keep in a plastic storage bag.

When ready to use, rub directly on the meat and allow to marinate for 2 to 3 hours in the refrigerator before cooking.

Barbecue and Sweet-and-Sour Sauces

BETTY'S BETTER BARBECUE SAUCE

Ingredients

1 cup ketchup

4 T. mustard

4 T. vinegar

4 T. sugar

4 T. Worcestershire sauce

1 tsp. kosher salt

Dash of hot sauce

Directions

Mix all ingredients together in a small pan and simmer for 15 minutes.

Cover and refrigerate overnight.

Pour over meat and simmer for one hour.

HOMEMADE BARBECUE SAUCE

Ingredients

3 T. butter, melted

1 medium onion, finely chopped

2 ribs celery, finely chopped

½ cup brown sugar

1 tsp. kosher salt

1 T. garlic powder

1 tsp. paprika

1 tsp. hot pepper sauce

1 tsp. dry mustard

2 cups ketchup

2 cups ginger ale

3 T. Worcestershire sauce

3 T. apple cider vinegar

¼ tsp. thyme

¼ tsp. marjoram

Directions

Mix all ingredients in a saucepan and simmer for 1 hour.

Cool and store in the refrigerator.

LINDSEY'S SWEET-AND-SOUR DRESSING

Ingredients

1 cup vegetable oil

1 cup sugar

½ cup wine vinegar

3 tsp. soy sauce

Dash of salt

Pepper to taste

Directions

Blend all ingredients well.

SWEET-AND-SOUR SAUCE

Ingredients

1 cup sugar

½ cup water

½ cup white vinegar

2 T. cornstarch + 1 tsp. water

2 T. ketchup

2 tsp. mustard

Directions

Combine the sugar, water, and vinegar in a saucepan. Cook until sugar is dissolved, about 5 minutes.

Mix cornstarch with 1 teaspoon of water. Add this to the hot sugar mixture and stir constantly until thickened. Remove from heat.

Let cool for 1 minute and add remaining ingredients.

SWEET-AND-SOUR SAUCE FOR VENISON AND OTHER MEATS

Ingredients

3 cups soup stock or water
   (if using water, add 2 T. sugar)

½ cup ketchup

¼ cup grated ginger

1 tsp. pepper

1 tsp. salt

2 T. sugar

2 T. vinegar

Directions

Put soup stock in a pot and heat to medium high. Add all other ingredients and bring to boil. Then put heat on low and simmer for 10 minutes.

TRADITIONAL SWEET-AND-SOUR SAUCE

Ingredients

2 tsp. cornstarch

4 tsp. water

⅓ cup rice vinegar

4 T. light brown sugar

1 T. ketchup

1 tsp. soy sauce

This sauce can be used hot or cold.

Directions

Mix the cornstarch with water until there are no lumps.

Combine all the ingredients in a small saucepan. Bring to a boil, stirring constantly. Let mixture bubble for 1 minute, making sure the sauce looks clear.

Dipping Sauces

HOMEMADE DIPPING SAUCE

Ingredients

½ cup mayonnaise

2 tsp. ketchup

2 T. grated horseradish

⅛ tsp. oregano

¼ tsp. kosher salt

¼ tsp. paprika

Black pepper to taste

⅛ tsp. cayenne pepper

Directions

Mix all ingredients in a bowl. Cool, cover, and store in the refrigerator.

SWEET RED ONION MARMALADE

Ingredients

2 cups sliced red onion (or sweet onion)

½ cup red wine

2 T. butter

½ cup red wine vinegar

½ cup sugar

Salt to taste

Directions

Combine all ingredients in a medium saucepan and stir well.

Simmer for 30 minutes over medium heat or until all liquid is cooked off and the onion is translucent.

HOMEMADE TARTAR SAUCE

Ingredients

1 cup mayonnaise

¼ cup finely diced onion

⅓ cup sweet pickle relish

¼ tsp. garlic powder

½ tsp. sugar

¼ tsp. marjoram

½ cup brown sugar

Directions

Mix all ingredients in a bowl. Cover and store in the refrigerator.

HOMEMADE COCKTAIL SAUCE

Ingredients

1 cup ketchup

1 T. fresh, grated horseradish

1 T. lemon juice

1 tsp. Worcestershire
    sauce

Directions

Mix all ingredients in a bowl. Cover and store in the refrigerator.

Part Eight

GRILLING

BANNED FROM THE BACKYARD GRILL

It was 1977 on a summer afternoon at our home in Nashville when my (Steve) Uncle Dan Chapman and his family arrived for a visit. His children were preteens, and when I asked if they were hungry they responded with an excited, belly-growling "Yes!"

Hearing the ravenous tone in our young guests' voices, Annie responded by doing something I've never gotten over. She handed me a bag of charcoal, a can of lighter fluid, a box of matches, and said, "Would you get the fire started and grill the hamburgers for us?"

"Sure thing, babe!" I answered as if I were a grill master. But the truth was, the only grilling I'd ever done was with my dad's old 1963 Biscayne Chevy when I accidentally "grilled" a dog on the highway on my way home from a high school football game. As for cooking freshly ground meat, I was a total novice. Still, I decided to give it a whirl.

I'd watched Annie build a little stack of briquettes on the grate of our little grill before, and I knew enough to douse them with lighter fluid, let the pile soak for a few minutes, and then put a flame to it. That part I managed quite well. However, when Annie brought the plate of nicely formed, uncooked burgers to me, she made the terrible mistake of assuming I had the know-how needed to use that flame to turn raw meat into something humans could consume. She should have known better.

I'll spare you all the pitiful details of what happened in the next several minutes, but here are a few ways I managed to do some serious burger bungling. I "wallered" those burgers all over the backyard. I tossed them on the grill and broke them. I lost sections of meat between the wires of the grate. I even dropped a couple on the grass. Not to be defeated or admit defeat, I quickly picked them up, wiped the grass clippings off, and put them back on the grill. Then, to top everything off, the dripping grease from the meat caused a flare-up of flame that nearly singed my eyebrows off. I looked like I'd been in a vicious fight with our dinner...and lost.

To make the situation worse, my Uncle Dan and his 12-year-old son stood by and watched me as I battled the beef, the grill, and everything else. They silently observed the fiasco. I appreciated them holding back on the comments so I could concentrate on the task at hand.

I finally got all the burgers back on the grill and pieced together. Though several were severely mangled and some contained flecks of grass and sand, at least they started to look done. I was just about ready to transfer them to a plate to deliver to Annie when Dan's boy couldn't hold back his fear any longer.

"Dad?" I could tell a question was about to follow by the way the boy talked and looked pleadingly at his dad.

"Yes, son?"

The youngster pointed at the meaty mess on the grill and said nervously, "Dad, are we gonna have to eat *that*?"

Right then and there I decided to never ever be in charge of grilling again. And that self-imposed ban is still in place today. I have not grilled since 1977! All the guests Annie and I have hosted at back-yard barbecues since then will never know how thankful they should be that I put such a policy in place.

Fortunately, when we want the taste of burgers cooked over an open flame and laced with the sweet smell of barbecue, Annie, Nathan, or our son-in-law Emmitt capably take charge. But even the three of them agreed that if this cookbook was going to contain helpful tips on how to manage a grill, there was only one real expert to go to. That person is my hunting buddy Lindsey Williams.

Lindsey is not only a skilled hunter, but we've tasted enough of his cooking exploits to report that he knows his way around the smoke pit. Because he's an expert at both "killin' and grillin' wild game," we asked him to share some back-yard barbecue how-tos.

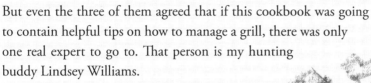

GRILLING TIPS

BY LINDSEY WILLIAMS

The Grill

- Choose a sturdy grill with good grill grates and a large enough cooking surface to meet your needs.

- A grill with a cover is best because it gives you more cooking options.

- I prefer a charcoal grill over a gas grill because cooking over coals gives more flavor to the food. There are benefits to using gas, such as easy temperature regulation and less steps in the "man make fire" process.

The Fire

- Hardwood lump charcoal is best because it gives food a more natural wood flavor. Hardwood lump charcoal also burns hotter than briquettes.

- Charcoal briquettes are manufactured with products that help bind the briquettes together. In my opinion, these impart a chemical taste to the food.

- Charcoal briquettes burn cooler than hardwood lump charcoal, but they last a bit longer.

- There are charcoal briquettes that will start by just striking a match to them. This type of charcoal gives the strongest chemical taste to whatever is being cooked. If you prefer the taste of petroleum to the taste of what you're cooking, this is the way to go.

- Propane gas grills are easy to light, and the cooking temps can be easily dialed in. But cooking over gas does not give the food the additional flavor that cooking with charcoal does.

- To start your charcoal, you can use lighter fluid or a charcoal chimney. Lighter fluid can be dangerous and leaves a petroleum flavor on what is being cooked. A charcoal chimney starter uses pieces of newspaper to start the coals, avoiding the lighter fluid flavor.

Grilling Tools

- Tongs and spatula for turning food
- Grilling grid or basket for fish or chopped vegetables
- Wire grill brush or stainless steel pads for cleaning grill
- Flame-retardant glove for handling hot coals and the grill
- Digital meat thermometer for making sure food is thoroughly cooked
- Spray bottle filled with water for spritzing and controlling flare-ups that blacken food

Grill Prep

- Once you have a good, hot fire going, close the grill lid to let the grates get good and hot.

- Then open the grill and use the wire grill brush to clean the grates.

- Before you put food on the grill, take a paper towel soaked in vegetable oil and brush it across the grill's cooking surface using tongs. This keeps the food from sticking to the grill.

- This is also the best time to arrange your fire into zones for direct and indirect cooking. For cooking directly over the coals, make sure the coals extend one inch beyond the surface the meat is going to cook over. For indirect cooking, make sure you have enough surface with no coals underneath to accommodate what you're grilling.

 **GRILLING: DIRECT AND INDIRECT**

- ***Direct Grilling:*** If the food will take less than 30 minutes to barbecue, cook directly over the coals. This includes burgers, steaks, fish, small or boneless pieces of fowl, and sausages.

- ***Indirect Grilling:*** Foods that take longer than 30 minutes to cook are best cooked over indirect heat. This works best for large cuts of meat like whole tenderloins, backstraps, and turkey breasts.

How-to Steps for Indirect Grilling

- Bank coals on one or both sides of a drip pan that will be placed on the lower grid.

- Sear meat over coals for a minute per side, and then move it to the center of grill over the drip pan.

- Close the grill to contain the heat and seal in the smoky flavor.

- Add apple juice or other flavored beverages to the drip pan, if desired, to provide moistness and flavor to the meat.

- If you want to add more smoke flavor, get wood chips (hickory, cherry, apple, mesquite, oak) and soak them in saltwater for at least 30 minutes. Then wrap the soaked wood chips in foil, punch holes in the top of the foil pouch, and place directly on top of the coals. Make sure you close the top of the grill when cooking to keep that good smoke flavor where the meat is.

GRILL MEAT PREPARATION

Wild game meat can be brined, marinated, or have a spice rub applied, depending on the kind of meat and what you want it to taste like.

- **_Brining_** makes cooked meat retain moisture. The salt in the brine solution causes the cells of the meat to absorb water via osmosis. The salt then causes the proteins to coagulate, which traps and holds the water molecules. This prevents the meat being grilled from drying out (as long as it's not overcooked). Brining works best on wild birds and hogs. Here's a simple brine recipe:

   To a large bowl of water add ½ cup kosher salt and ¼ cup sugar. You may also add any fresh (not dried) herbs, such as thyme and rosemary. Crushed juniper berries are a good addition too. Put the meat into the brine and let it sit in the refrigerator for 2 to 3 hours for smaller cuts of meat.

- **_Marinating_** is soaking meat in a seasoned liquid before cooking to add flavor and tenderize. The liquid, or marinade, is usually acidic and contains ingredients such as vinegar, lemon juice, or wine. A marinade often includes oils, herbs, or other spices to add more flavor. The process may last minutes, as in the case of fish, or hours depending on the type and size of the cuts of meat. Check out the Gravies, Marinades, and Sauces section starting on page 184. Here's a simple marinade for red meat, such as venison, elk, and bison:

   ¼ cup soy sauce, ¼ cup olive oil, 2 T. ketchup, 2 T. red wine vinegar, 2 T. minced garlic, 1 T. freshly ground black pepper. Mix all ingredients and pour over red meat in a freezer bag. Let meat marinate for 6 to 8 hours, turning every now and then to make sure all of meat gets covered.

- **_Spice rub_** is a mixture of ground spices created to add flavor to meat. Sometimes salt is added for flavor, and sugar is included to cause the rub to caramelize. The simplest rub is just coarsely ground black pepper. The spices are rubbed on the meat before cooking, forming a coating. For the flavors to permeate the meat, the rub needs to be on the meat for several hours before cooking. If you want a crust on the meat or just have the outer portion of the meat flavored, begin cooking immediately after the meat has been coated. So apply the following rub 12 to 24 hours before cooking or just before meat goes on the grill. The longer the rub is on the meat before cooking, the more the meat will be flavored by the spices. The spices are usually coarsely ground.

GRILLING WILD GAME

- Allow meat to come to room temperature before cooking.

- Wild game is extremely lean and will cook faster than you think. Use a digital thermometer frequently to check the internal temperature of the meat. Overcooking makes wild game dry and tough—think shoe leather.

- Wild game should be cooked to a temperature 10 to 15 degrees less than domestic meat. For example, domestic turkey is done when the thermometer registers 165º to 175º. Wild turkey is well-done at 160º.

- Always take game off the grill when it's 5 to 10 degrees before fully cooked status (as shown on the thermometer). Allow it to stand for at least 5 minutes before serving. During this time the internal temperature of the meat will continue to rise. (Yes, it's still cooking, folks!) Letting it stand helps the meat retain more juices.

Recipe Index

ACKNOWLEDGMENTS

We want to thank these folks for their contributions:

Willie B
Emmitt and Heidi Beall
Chuck and Kathy Bentley
Kenneth and Evelyn Bledsoe
Carey Bratusek
Travis Cadle
Paul J. and Lillian Chapman
Curt and Delight Christman
Karl and Alice Click
Bobby Emfinger
Joe and Ginny Emmert
Karen Fletcher
Christie (Bonecutter) Francis
Rhoda Grace
JJ Hankins
Joel and LaBreeska Hemphill
Don and Doris Hicks

Jan Leary
Chuck Loebsack
James Mayo
Mary Jean Murphy
Randy and Dena Petrich
    (www.hunginginmontana.com)
George Reidel
Donnie (Boog) Reynolds
Bob Roberts
Kay Dekalb Smith
Donnie Tyndall
Lindsey and Susan Williams
    (http://thatsusanwilliams.com)

And a special thanks to
David R. Quick

ABOUT THE AUTHORS

Steve and Annie Chapman are award-winning musicians who take their message of Christ-centered family to fans all over North America. Steve's books include *365 Things Every Hunter Should Know* and *A Look at Life from the Fairway*.

ENJOY MORE THAN 200 WHOLESOME AND DELICIOUS RECIPES FEATURING TURKEY, FISH, VENISON, ELK, AND MORE EXOTIC WILD GAME TO PLEASE EVEN THE MOST ADVENTUROUS PALETTES.

HAVE YOU BEEN HUNTING FOR NEW WAYS TO SERVE WILD GAME?

From the kitchen of the bestselling author of *A Look at Life from a Deer Stand*, Steve Chapman, and his wife Annie, here is a collection of hearty, homemade family favorites. The Chapmans also share hunting recipes and stories from their friends and family, along with great ideas for sauces, side dishes, and desserts, so you can create memorable meals for your friends and family.

Steve and **Annie Chapman** are award-winning musicians who take their message of Christ-centered family to fans all over North America. Steve's books include *365 Things Every Hunter Should Know* and *A Look at Life from the Fairway*.

TEN PEAKS PRESS®

Cookbook
ISBN 978-0-7369-8899-5 U.S. $26.99